Acclaim for A N D R E   D U B U S 's

Meditations from a Movable Chair

"Emotionally intense . . . Dubus presents his memories and meditations like panes in a stained glass window held up against the light of his own passion and conviction."
—*Chicago Tribune*

"Graceful, dignified . . . the exquisite rhythms of Dubus's sentences are matched by no one else writing today."   —*Time Out*

"Beautiful as a view is beautiful, or a child, or a righteous struggle with a victorious ending."
—*Los Angeles Times*

"Overwhelming . . . often inspiring . . . [Dubus] cuts to the heart of things without pretense."
—*The Washington Post*

"Andre Dubus's rousing assembly of observations and considerations about pride in—and detachment from—the body . . . is as strong and honest as an oak."   —*Esquire*

ALSO BY ANDRE DUBUS

The Lieutenant

Separate Flights

Adultery & Other Choices

Finding a Girl in America

The Times Are Never So Bad

Voices from the Moon

The Last Worthless Evening

Selected Stories

Broken Vessels (nonfiction)

Dancing After Hours

ANDRE DUBUS

Meditations from a Movable Chair

The author of nine works of fiction, Andre Dubus received the PEN/Malamud Award, the Rea Award for excellence in short fiction, the Jean Stein Award from the American Academy of Arts and Letters, the *Boston Globe*'s first annual Lawrence L. Winship Award, and fellowships from both the Guggenheim and MacArthur Foundations. Until his death in 1999, he lived in Haverhill, Massachusetts.

Meditations from a Movable Chair

ESSAYS BY

Andre Dubus

VINTAGE CONTEMPORARIES
Vintage Books
A Division of Random House, Inc.
New York

FIRST VINTAGE CONTEMPORARIES EDITION, APRIL 1999

Some of the essays in this work were originally published in the following: "Carrying" and "Messages" in the *Boston Globe Sunday Magazine;* "Love in the Morning" in *DoubleTake;* "Song of Pity" and "Digging" in *Epoch;* "Imperiled Men" in *Harper's;* "About Kathryn" in *Health Magazine;* "A Hemingway Story" in *The Kenyon Review;* "First Books" in Ken Lopez's *Catalogue of First Books;* "Giving up the Gun" and "Witness" in *The New Yorker;* "Sacraments," "Communion," and "Girls" in *Portland Magazine;* "Brothers" in *Salon;* "Mailer at the Algonquin" in *The Sewanee Review;* "Legs," "Grace," and "Autumn Legs" in *The Southern Review;* "Bodily Mysteries" in *Special Report;* "A Country Road Song" and "Liv Ullmann in Spring" in *Yankee;* "Good-bye to Richard Yates" in *Richard Yates, An American Writer: Tributes in Memoriam,* published by Seymour Lawrence.

The Library of Congress has cataloged the Alfred A. Knopf edition as follows:
Dubus, Andre, [date]
Meditations from a movable chair : essays / by Andre Dubus
p. cm.
ISBN 0-679-43108-X (alk. paper)
1. Dubus, Andre, [date]—Biography. 2. Novelists, American—20th century—Biography. I. Title.
PS3554.U265Z47 1998
813'.54—dc21   97-50551 CIP [B]

Vintage ISBN: 0-679-75115-7

www.vintagebooks.com

Printed in the United States of America
10 9 8 7 6 5 4 3 2 1

I thank the late Michael Rea, and Elizabeth Rea, and Frieda Arkin, and Scott Downing, and the Thursday Nighters.—A. D.

To Marion Ettlinger and Joseph Hurka

"Continue, slowly, and wait for luck to change."
—Ernest Hemingway,
"The Gambler, the Nun,
and the Radio"

"And where are the windows? Where does the light come in? . . . Maybe the light is going to have to come in as best it can, through whatever chinks and cracks have been left in the builder's faulty craftsmanship, and if that's the case you can be sure that nobody feels worse about it than I do. God knows, Bernie; God knows there certainly ought to be a window around here somewhere, for all of us."
—Richard Yates,
"Builders"

Contents

CONTENTS

Meditations from a

Movable Chair

About Kathryn

YOU HAVE TO KNOW WHAT IT'S LIKE down there. In Louisiana winter, my father played golf every weekend, unless a lot of rain was falling; you can work up a sweat just carrying a golf bag on that flat land. If you want to, you can go into the rice fields or swamps or the woods near the bayou and scare up a cottonmouth. No need to wait for the long hot summer. If you're a woman, you can be raped on your lawn two nights after Christmas, like my sister Kathryn.

She tells me about it on the phone. Two nights after Christmas is a Friday. After work at the bank, she goes to the gym, where she reads on the treadmill. On the way home, she stops to buy coffee.

"Maybe that's where he saw me," she says on the phone. She is long divorced, and has eight grown children and four grandchildren. A daughter lives with her. She gets a pound of rich dark coffee and walks into the lulling winter air and the beginning of her weekend. She drives to her street, one flanked by houses, and when she turns onto it, she sees in her rearview mirror a car turning behind her.

She is a calm woman. Yet an instinct tells her to drive past her house. But now she is home, and she turns into the driveway, where her daughter's car is parked. She drives behind the house, and stops on a concrete slab there, near the back door. The instinct is quelled. She cannot see the front of her house now, nor most of the driveway. She takes a while leaving the car, getting her gym bag and purse and the bag with the coffee. She carries these to the back door; then he is there: a large black man holding a knife, and saying, "Give me your money." She tells him she has only five dollars, and gives him her wallet. He asks how much is in the house. She says there is nothing in the house. She can feel her daughter in there. To his questions, she answers: Yes, she is married; he is at work; he gets off at seven. She knows it is now around seven-thirty.

The man takes her arm and pulls her around to the side of the house. He removes her glasses, flings them. Her neighbors' house is near. The rape commences, and she thinks how silly this is, to die in her own yard. She no longer sees the knife, and she waits for it. He is talking and she says, "What?" and she hears "Oral sex" and says, "No"; and, to God, she says silently: Don't You dare do this to me. It doesn't happen. She lies beneath his heavy weight. He hears something in the house: maybe the shower, maybe her daughter's footsteps. He says: "Who's in the house?"

"My daughter." Knowing, oh Lord, the wrong image came to her brain, the wrong words to her tongue. But how cunning can she be? He is raping her, she is waiting for a blade to slash or pierce her body, and she is as conscious of her daughter's body as she is of her own. What other words can she speak? The fabricated husband was long ago, when she was still standing, still wearing gym pants and underwear; he has been shocked out of her mind. Who is in the house? My daughter. Whom are you trying to protect? My daughter. Whose face, whose name, whose body fills your heart and mind, right now? My daughter.

"Want me to go fuck her too?"

"Don't you *dare*. Listen. I got paid today. We can go get it."

"Where?"

"In the checking account. In the machine."

"How far is it?"

"Just a mile."

He stops raping her. He stands. She is spared his ejaculation, and later she will be grateful for that.

She stands and pulls up her sweatpants, and covers herself.

"You'll have to get my glasses. I can't see a thing."

He gets on his hands and knees, and crawls. Then she is screaming and running, away from her daughter, to her neighbors' house. As she reaches the front door, a woman opens it and Kathryn hears his car. He is leaving, he is gone.

"He was such a jerk," my sister says on the phone. In Massachusetts, I sit in my wheelchair and listen; I see her face as though she is in the room.

"I said God bless you to him," she says. "While it was going on." I think of Christ nailed to wood, my sister spiked to the earth of her lawn. "I prayed for him Sunday, at Mass."

She says if he had raped her daughter, she would have killed him. I try to imagine her killing a big man. I can. I know a woman whose small son was sinking in mud at the beach. Wooden pallets were stacked on the wharf; she laid them in a line to her son, crawled out on them, and saved him. When she tried to return the pallets, she could not lift one of them.

"I'd like him castrated," she says.

She has been telling people about it. She wants women to know, and to take care. A young man at the bank said: "You're *telling* people? There's a *stigma* to that." My sister said: "What stigma? *I* didn't do anything." As she tells her story, she hears others, from women. Darkness envelops her: she is on a prairie over a hundred years ago, in the long cold night; and sheltered by her roof and walls, she listens for a footstep at her door. She says: "I hate this world we live in now."

"So do I."

When we were children, we once lived in a house with a fig tree in the backyard. One spring, a mockingbird had a nest there and, if we got near the tree, she dived and screamed at us. My sisters and I picked figs in the morning. Sometimes milky liquid from the fig leaves made our skin itch. The figs were lovely. Our mother peeled them and we ate them with cream and sugar. In July, she made preserves, the figs unpeeled and dark and sweet in winter, and we ate them with biscuits and eggs. It was a large fig tree, its branches low, near the ground, and I liked climbing it, and lying under it on my back, looking up at the trunk and branches and leaves and the sky. The branches were so low that someone standing in the yard could not see me. It was a good place to be nine years old, smelling grass and leaves and figs under the hot blue sky.

Kathryn was fifteen then. One summer night, our parents went out, leaving her in charge of my sister Beth and me. In our family, all of us kissed good morning, good-bye after breakfast, hello when we came home, and good night before going to bed. That evening, I was in the backyard when

my parents left. I heard the car doors, Daddy closing Mother's after she got in, then moments later
his own. I ran to the driveway for my kisses, but my
parents were gone. I went inside and said to my sisters: "They didn't kiss me good-bye."

"They couldn't find you," one of them said.
"They called you."

I went out the back door and crawled under the
fig tree and lay facedown on the grass and cried.
It was twilight, and I was still crying when I heard
the screen door open and close, and I shamefully
looked out at Kathryn and stopped crying and
wiped my eyes. But she was not looking for me. She
walked slowly past the tree and stopped at the edge
of our lawn and a neighbor's garden. The moon
was up, pale in the fading light, and she looked at
it and began to weep. My own sadness left me. I lay
still and watched her crying and wondered at the
sorrow of being my fifteen-year-old sister. The sky
was dark when she wiped away her tears and went
inside. I stayed under the tree for a while longer,
then went into the house. I did not tell her for
thirty years or more. We were a mother and father
then, and divorced. She did not remember the
night, or why she was crying.

Now I think of her praying for the man who
raped her; saying she would have killed him if he
had raped her daughter; praying for him; wanting
him castrated; praying for him; calling him a jerk.
He is gone from her flesh, and she is cleansing her

soul; she prays so she can forgive him. It is hard work and will take a long time. But one bright day her anger and hatred will burn to white ash, and she will forgive him, the rape will finally end, and the man will be truly gone, to wander in her past. This is my sister who wept near the fig tree and grew into a woman who would have killed for her daughter, and who gave God's blessing to the man who came with a knife out of the darkness.

Legs

THIS WAS LONG AGO, OR WHAT FEELS like long ago. I had two strong legs then. A young woman I knew disliked her thighs. She believed they were too large. Her body was small, and she was athletic, and I told her she could not lose weight from only her thighs. She was nineteen, and was running two miles a day. I was forty-one and sometimes I ran with her. One day, we ran five miles; she had never run that far, and I teased her about her youth, my age. We ran on a country road past houses, a large pond, and long stretches of woods. In my car, I had measured this road; I knew at which house or curve or hill each new mile began. Sometimes we drove to a lake where a five-and-a-half-mile dirt trail went around the water, through woods, and up long hills. On one of my birthdays, we ran eleven miles; I used to do that on my birthdays in August, with my oldest son.

One day when she was sad about her thighs, I said to her: You have wonderful legs: "I've seen you run, swim, water-ski, cross-country ski, dance; and you ski downhill. You should be grateful that you have your legs." I do not remember ever feeling grateful for mine. For over two decades before I met this woman, I ran for the joy and catharsis of it, and I used to say I had legs like trees.

Letter to a Writers' Workshop

A writers' workshop has met in my home on Thursday nights since the fall of 1987. Writers come for a few months or years, then leave, and someone else comes. In June of 1992, Christopher Tilghman and Jim Thompson, who had been members of the workshop since its beginning, came to my house so we could talk about what we were doing on Thursday nights. We were not doing well; I was a poor leader. Afterward, I wrote this letter to the writers.

CHRIS AND JIM AND I TALKED ABOUT writing, and reading to people, and listening to what people say. We have twelve passionate writers and, quite naturally and quite morally, when we hear stories, we talk about them. I've felt for some time that we talk more than we should, because we only hear the stories, we do not read them, and cannot possibly, as a group, be accurate. It has taken me a long time to admit that I generally miss a page or two when I'm hearing a story. A good line or image sometimes stimulates me so, absorbs me so, that I simply don't hear the next page. We've tried giving copies to everyone to read, and it's too much to ask or receive. We'd like to meet now, beginning the Thursday after Labor Day, for pleasure and encouragement. Chris said: "We're listening as writers; we should listen as readers."

So we'd like to have two readers a night, and limit discussions to fifteen minutes. That gives everyone time to say what, in general, is good about a story, and what needs work. This is a way of getting twelve people away from a writer's desk, of setting writers free to find editors they can trust. After I've read on Thursday nights, I've spent an inordinate amount of time—days, weeks, more— trying to reclaim my story or essay at my desk, get it back from all those voices I respect. Over the past year or more, those voices have been with me as I write, and I've had to concentrate more, to get rid of them. I've always thought of someone while writing, from time to time, testing a line on that person's eye (not ear): Chekhov, and wives and girlfriends. I'm sharing this with you because other writers in the group have shared the same experience with me. I like Chris's idea: call it a reading group, not a workshop. Perhaps workshops are better when they consist of ten or fewer rookies and one veteran whose job is to draw from the rookies whatever is there.

When I say we talk too much, I do not mean it in the usual sense. I mean there is too much light in the room, it dazzles, and most discussions last year left me drawn and quartered of spirit. I mean discussions of other people's work as well as my own. And what else can we expect when we read to eleven people whose vocation it is to write? We respond as writers, we rewrite stories by saying how they could be done differently, and very often we are talking about the way each of us would write the story, or a scene or passage in it. Even when we are right, there are too many of us. Certainly twelve people can disagree and all be right about how a story could be written. "The Short Happy Life of Francis Macomber" would not have survived us without a stubborn author. I mention that story because I can read it in two absolutely different ways: if I take the title as ironic, I like the story, for it shows the foolishness of these folk; if I take the title seriously, I don't like the story. I've talked to a lot of writers over the decades about this story, and confusion abounds. Thomas Williams, God bless him, said it best: "It's either one of Hemingway's best stories or one of his worst, depending on how you read it."

And, oh, what is important is that Hemingway wrote it and we can read it, and if he made mistakes, if he left things unclear, well, that's better than scurrying home to revise and revise and revise and make it clear for everyone. Because no one knows where the words are coming from anyway, no one writing sincerely (Nadine Gordimer defined *sincerity* in *My Son's Story* as "never speaking from an idea of oneself"); no one knows where the images and the very story are coming from. We sit at the desk and try to concentrate absolutely, and concentration takes us to the place where the words and images and stories are. This is not a place we can reach every time we want to; it is a strange place; and, very often, reading galleys of my work, I have found a sentence difficult to understand, as though someone else had written it; and, very often too, I have been surprised by feelings of a character, and the revelations in the character's spirit. This summer, I read *Peace Is Every Step* by Thich Nhat Hanh, a Buddhist monk, and as I read of what he calls "mindfulness," I realized why writing and physical exercise have been so deeply pleasurable for me despite or because of the effort they demand: while doing both of those, if I am concentrating, I am one with the man I normally am not and, achieving or receiving that, I am one with people and truths I will never know when I am my normal self again: driving a car, or watching men throw a baseball, or talking with friends.

And to achieve or receive these truths on the

page, each of us has to proceed alone, in our own way, and very often that way is a clumsy one. At the Iowa Writers' Workshop, Richard Yates taught us *From Here to Eternity*, a novel he loved. Yates said to us: "If Jones had been in a workshop here, I would have said: 'You know, Jim, your first chapter reads like the first chapter of a short book; but this is a very long book, so I think you ought to rewrite that first chapter'; and a year from now, I'd say, 'How's the revision of that first chapter going?' and he'd say, 'Oh swell, Dick, swell,' and he'd keep on writing his great book." Toby Wolff heard me read a story in Ohio, where we were working together for a few summer days, and afterward, over drinks, he said: "I think at the end you played the organ just a little too long." I not only knew precisely what he meant but I agreed, and I knew he would have written the end better, and as a reader I would have enjoyed it more; and I knew that I wouldn't change what I had written, because that was the only way I could write it, and if I changed it, it wouldn't be mine anymore. We can't make them perfectly, only as best as we can. Hemingway once said that he had very little natural talent and what people called his style was simply his effort to overcome his lack of talent. Don't take that lightly. What is art if not a concentrated and impassioned effort to make something with the little we have, the little we see?

We shall remain flexible. This is a talented and generous group, and everyone will be served.

Some I've spoken to feel the need, at times, for more extensive criticism; they will give us manuscripts to take home and read; then we can meet to discuss the story, rather than listen to it. One writer I've spoken to feels more free this summer, "writing alone," and would like to choose someone else's story to read to us. I'd love to read Chekhov's "A Woman's Kingdom," which I read again this summer; it is one of the most magnificent stories I've ever read, but it's forty-seven pages long in a Modern Library edition, so probably eighty in manuscript, and would take too long.

People who want to read work in progress must be extremely stubborn; a little hearing impairment would be helpful. We've been at least potentially lethal in the past, and I'm impressed by Edie Clark's tenacity: finishing her book after those long discussions of its sections. I don't believe I would have been able to.

If Hemingway in his thirties were among us, would there really be any more to say after he read than: "Ernest, this is beautiful writing, you took me to Africa, Francis and Margot and Wilson are real, it's an exciting story, but Ernest: Am I supposed to feel that Francis is a foolish boy in a man's body doing foolish things in Africa? Or do you want me to believe Francis actually had a breakthrough?" Or, as a young female student of mine years ago said: "He had to end that story with Francis getting killed because, believe me, when they got back to

New York it was going to be the same old stuff again, she was going to cheat on him again, and he'd be a wimp again. . . ."

And so it goes. Beautiful, isn't it? "It's what they call flesh we're in. And a fine old dance it is" (Christopher Fry wrote that), and we're not going to understand it all in one Thursday evening in Haverhill, Massachusetts, so let's listen to stories and be honest but try to stay general rather than specific, and let the mysteries go home with the writer.

Digging

T HAT HOT JUNE IN LAFAYETTE, LOUI-
siana, I was sixteen, I would be seventeen in
August, I weighed one hundred and five pounds,
and my ruddy, broad-chested father wanted me to
have a summer job. I only wanted the dollar al-
lowance he gave me each week, and the dollar and
a quarter I earned caddying for him on weekends and Wednesday afternoons. With a quarter I
could go to a movie, or buy a bottle of beer, or a
pack of cigarettes to smoke secretly. I did not have
a girlfriend, so I did not have to buy drinks or food
or movie tickets for anyone else. I did not want to
work. I wanted to drive around with my friends, or

walk with them downtown, to stand in front of the department store, comb our ducktails, talk, look at girls.

My father was a civil engineer, and the district manager for the Gulf States Utilities Company. He had been working for them since he left college, beginning as a surveyor, wearing boots and khakis and, in a holster on his belt, a twenty-two-caliber pistol for cottonmouths. At home he was quiet; in the evenings he sat in his easy chair, and smoked, and read: *Time, The Saturday Evening Post, Collier's, The Reader's Digest*, detective novels, books about golf, and Book of the Month Club novels. He loved to talk, and he did this at parties I listened to from my bedroom, and with his friends on the golf course, and drinking in the clubhouse after playing eighteen holes. I listened to more of my father's conversations about politics and golf and his life and the world than I ever engaged in during the nearly twenty-two years I lived with him. I was afraid of angering him, seeing his blue eyes, and reddening face, hearing the words he would use to rebuke me; but what I feared most was his voice, suddenly and harshly rising. He never yelled for long, only a few sentences, but they emptied me, as if his voice had pulled my soul from my body. His voice seemed to empty the house too and, when he stopped yelling, the house filled with silence. He did not yell often. That sound was not part of our family life. The fear of it was part of my love for him.

I was shy with him. Since my forties, I have believed that he was shy with me too, and I hope it was not as painful for him as it was for me. I think my shyness had very little to do with my fear. Other boys had fathers who yelled longer and more often, fathers who spanked them or, when they were in their teens, slapped or punched them. My father spanked me only three times, probably because he did not know of most of my transgressions. My friends with harsher fathers were neither afraid nor shy; they quarreled with their fathers, provoked them. My father sired a sensitive boy, easily hurt or frightened, and he worried about me; I knew he did when I was a boy, and he told me this on his deathbed, when I was a Marine captain.

My imagination gave me a dual life: I lived in my body, and at the same time lived a life no one could see. All my life, I have told myself stories, and have talked in my mind to friends. Imagine my father sitting at supper with my mother and two older sisters and me: I am ten and small and appear distracted. Every year at school, there is a bully, sometimes a new one, sometimes the one from the year before. I draw bullies to me, not because I am small, but because they know I will neither fight nor inform on them. I will take their pushes or pinches or punches, and try not to cry, and I will pretend I am not hurt. My father does not know this. He only sees me at supper, and I am not there. I am riding a horse and shooting bad men. My father eats, glances at me. I know he is trying to see who I am, who I will be.

Before my teens, he took me to professional wrestling matches because I wanted to go; he told me they were fake, and I did not believe him. We listened to championship boxing matches on the radio. When I was not old enough to fire a shotgun, he took me dove hunting with his friends: we crouched in a ditch facing a field, and I watched the doves fly toward us and my father rising to shoot; then I ran to fetch the warm, dead, and delicious birds. In summer, he took me fishing with his friends; we walked in woods to creeks and bayous and fished with bamboo poles. When I was ten, he learned to play golf and stopped hunting and fishing, and on weekends I was his caddy. I did not want to be, I wanted to play with my friends, but when I became a man and left home, I was grateful that I had spent those afternoons watching him, listening to him. A minor-league baseball team made our town its home, and my father took me to games, usually with my mother. When I was twelve or so, he taught me to play golf, and sometimes I played nine holes with him; more often and more comfortably, I played with other boys.

If my father and I were not watching or listening to something and responding to it, or were not doing something, but were simply alone together, I could not talk, and he did not, and I felt that I should, and I was ashamed. That June of my seventeenth year, I could not tell him that I did not want a job. He talked to a friend of his, a building contractor, who hired me as a carpenter's helper; my pay was seventy-five cents an hour.

On a Monday morning, my father drove me to work. I would ride the bus home and, next day, would start riding the bus to work. Probably my father drove me that morning because it was my first day; when I was twelve, he had taken me to a store to buy my first pair of long pants; we boys wore shorts and, in fall and winter, knickers and long socks till we were twelve; and he had taken me to a barber for my first haircut. In the car, I sat frightened, sadly resigned, and feeling absolutely incompetent. I had the lunch my mother had put in a brown paper bag, along with a mason jar with sugar and squeezed lemons in it, so I could make lemonade with water from the cooler. We drove to a street with houses and small stores and parked at a corner where, on a flat piece of land, men were busy. They were building a liquor store, and I assumed I would spend my summer handing things to a carpenter. I hoped he would be patient and kind.

As a boy in Louisiana's benevolent winters and hot summers, I had played outdoors with friends: we built a clubhouse, chased one another on bicycles, shot air rifles at birds, tin cans, bottles, trees; in fall and winter, wearing shoulder pads and helmets, we played football on someone's very large side lawn; and in summer we played baseball in a field that a father mowed for us; he also built us a backstop of wood and chicken wire. None of us played well enough to be on a varsity team; but I wanted that gift, not knowing that it was a gift, and I felt ashamed that I did not have it. Now we drove cars, smoked, drank in nightclubs. This was French Catholic country; we could always buy drinks. Sometimes we went on dates with girls, but more often we looked at them and talked about them; or visited them, when several girls were gathered at the home of a girl whose parents were out for the evening. I had never done physical work except caddying, pushing a lawn mower, and raking leaves, and I was walking from the car with my father toward workingmen. My father wore his straw hat and seersucker suit. He introduced me to the foreman and said: "Make a man of him."

Then he left. The foreman wore a straw hat and looked old; everyone looked old; the foreman was probably thirty-five. I stood mutely, waiting for him to assign me to some good-hearted Cajun carpenter. He assigned me a pickax and a shovel and told me to get into the trench and go to work. In all four sides of the trench were files of black men, swinging picks and shoveling. The trench was about three feet deep and it would be the building's foundation; I went to where the foreman pointed, and laid my tools on the ground; two black men made a space for me, and I jumped between them. They smiled and we greeted one another. I would learn days later that they earned a dollar an hour.

They were men with families and I knew this was unjust, as everything else was for black people. But on that first morning, I did not know what they were being paid, I did not know their names, only that one was working behind me and one in front, and they were good to me and stronger than I could ever be. All I really knew in those first hours under the hot sun was raising the pickax and swinging it down, raising it and swinging, again and again till the earth was loose; then putting the pick on the ground beside me and taking the shovel and plunging it into dirt that I lifted and tossed beside the trench.

I did not have the strength for this: not in my back, my legs, my arms, my shoulders. Certainly not in my soul. I only wanted it to end. The air was very humid, and sweat dripped on my face and arms, soaked my shirt and jeans. My hands gripping the pick or shovel were sore, my palms burned, the muscles in my arms ached, and my breath was quick. Sometimes I saw tiny black spots before my eyes. Weakly, I raised the pick, straightening my back, then swung it down, bending my body with it, and it felt heavier than I was, more durable, this thing of wood and steel that was melting me. I laid it on the ground and picked up the shovel and pushed it into the dirt, lifted it, grunted, and emptied it beside the trench. The sun, always my friend till now, burned me, and my mouth and throat were dry, and often I climbed out of the trench and went to the large tin water-cooler with a block of ice in it and water from a hose. At the cooler were paper cups and salt tablets, and I swallowed salt and drank and drank, and poured water onto my head and face; then I went back to the trench, the shovel, the pick.

Nausea came in the third or fourth hour. I kept swinging the pick, pushing and lifting the shovel. I became my sick, hot, tired, and hurting flesh. Or it became me; so, for an hour or more, I tasted a very small piece of despair. At noon in Lafayette, a loud whistle blew, and in the cathedral the bell rang. I could not hear the bell where we worked, but I heard the whistle, and lowered the shovel and looked around. I was dizzy and sick. All the men had stopped working and were walking toward shade. One of the men with me said it was time to eat, and I climbed out of the trench and walked with the black men to the shade of the toolshed. The white men went to another shaded place; I do not remember what work they had been doing that morning, but it was not with picks and shovels in the trench. Everyone looked hot but comfortable. The black men sat talking and began to eat and drink. My bag of lunch and jar with lemons and sugar were on the ground in the shade. Still I stood, gripped by nausea. I looked at the black men and at my lunch bag. Then my stomach tightened and everything in it rose, and I went around the corner of the shed where no one could see me and, bending over, I vomited and moaned and heaved until it ended. I went to the watercooler and rinsed my mouth and spat, and then I took another paper cup and drank. I walked back to the shade and lay on my back, tasting vomit. One of the black men said: "You got to eat."

"I threw up," I said, and closed my eyes and slept for the rest of the hour that everyone—students and workers—had for the noon meal. At home, my nineteen-year-old sister and my mother and father were eating dinner, meat and rice and gravy, vegetables and salad and iced tea with a leaf of mint; and an oscillating fan cooled them. My twenty-two-year-old sister was married. At one o'clock, the whistle blew, and I woke up and stood and one of the black men said: "Are you all right?"

I nodded. If I had spoken, I might have wept. When I was a boy, I could not tell a man what I felt, if I believed what I felt was unmanly. We went back to the trench, down into it, and I picked up the shovel I had left there at noon, and shoveled out all the loose earth between me and the man in front of me, then put the shovel beside the trench, lifted the pick, raised it over my shoulder, and swung it down into the dirt. I was dizzy and weak and hot; I worked for forty minutes or so; then, above me, I heard my father's voice, speaking my name. I looked up at him; he was there to take me home, to forgive my failure, and in my great relief I could not know that I would not be able to forgive it. I was going home. But he said: "Let's go buy you a hat."

Every man there wore a hat, most of them straw,

the others baseball caps. I said nothing. I climbed out of the trench and went with my father. In the car, in a voice softened with pride, he said: "The foreman called me. He said the Nigras told him you threw up, and didn't eat, and you didn't tell him."

"That's right," I said, and shamefully watched the road, and cars with people who seemed free of all torment, and let my father believe I was brave, because I was afraid to tell him that I was afraid to tell the foreman. Quietly, we drove to town and he parked and took me first to a drugstore with air conditioning and a lunch counter, and bought me a 7UP for my stomach, and told me to order a sandwich. Sweet-smelling women at the counter were smoking. The men in the trench had smoked while they worked, but my body's only desire had been to stop shoveling and swinging the pick, to be, with no transition at all, in the shower at home, then to lie on my bed, feeling the soft breath of the fan on my damp skin. I would not have smoked at work anyway, with men. Now I wanted a cigarette. My father smoked, and I ate a bacon and lettuce and tomato sandwich.

Then we walked outside, into humidity and the heat and glare of the sun. We crossed the street to the department store, where, in the work-clothes section, my father chose a pith helmet. I did not want to wear a pith helmet. I would happily wear one in Africa, hunting lions and rhinoceroses. But I did not want to wear such a thing in Lafayette. I said nothing; there was no hat I wanted to wear. I carried the helmet in its bag out of the store and, in the car, laid it beside me. At that place where sweating men worked, I put it on; a thin leather strap looped around the back of my head. I went to my two comrades in the trench. One of them said: "That's a good hat."

I jumped in.

The man behind me said: "You going to be all right now."

I was; and I still do not know why. A sandwich and a soft drink had not given me any more strength than the breakfast I had vomited. An hour's respite in the car and the cool drugstore and buying the helmet that now was keeping my wet head cool certainly helped. But I had the same soft arms and legs, the same back and shoulders I had demanded so little of in my nearly seventeen years of stewardship. Yet all I remember of that afternoon is the absence of nausea.

At five o'clock, the whistle blew downtown and we climbed out of the trench and washed our tools with the hose, then put them in the shed. Dirt was on my arms and hands, my face and neck and clothes. I could have wrung sweat from my shirt and jeans. I got my lunch from the shade, my two comrades said: "See you tomorrow," and I said I would see them. I went to the bus stop at the corner and sat on the bench. My wet clothes cooled my skin. I looked down at my dirty tennis shoes; my socks and feet were wet. I watched people in passing cars. In one were teenaged boys, and they laughed and shouted something about my helmet. I watched the car till it was blocks away, then took off the helmet and held it on my lap. I carried it aboard the bus; yet all summer I wore it at work, maybe because my father bought it for me and I did not want to hurt him, maybe because it was a wonderful helmet for hard work outdoors in Louisiana.

My father got home before I did and told my mother and sister the story, the only one he knew, or the only one I assumed he knew. The women proudly greeted me when I walked into the house. They were also worried. They wanted to know how I felt. They wore dresses, they smelled of perfume or cologne, they were drinking bourbon and water, and my sister and father were smoking cigarettes. Standing in the living room, holding my lunch and helmet, I said I was fine. I could not tell the truth to these women who loved me, even if my father were not there. I could not say that I was not strong enough and that I could not bear going back to work tomorrow, and all summer, any more than I could tell them I did not believe I was as good at being a boy as other boys were: not at sports, or with girls; and now not with a man's work. I was home, where vases held flowers, and things were clean, and our manners were good.

Next morning, carrying my helmet and lunch, I rode the bus to work and joined the two black men in the trench. I felt that we were friends. Soon I felt this about all the black men at work. We were digging the foundation; we were the men and the boy with picks and shovels in the trench. One day, the foundation was done. I use the passive voice, because this was a square or rectangular trench, men were working at each of its sides, I had been working with my comrades on the same side for weeks, moving not forward but down. Then it was done. Someone told us. Maybe the contractor was there, with the foreman. Who dug out that last bit of dirt? I only knew that I had worked as hard as I could, I was part of the trench, it was part of me, and it was finished; it was there in the earth to receive concrete and probably never to be seen again. Someone should have blown a bugle; we should have climbed exultant from the trench, gathered to wipe sweat from our brows, drink water, shake hands, then walk together to each of the four sides and marvel at what we had made.

On that second morning of work, I was not sick, and at noon I ate lunch with the blacks in the shade; then we all slept on the grass till one o'clock. We worked till five, said good-bye to one another, and they went to the colored section of town, and I rode the bus home. When I walked into the living room, into cocktail hour, and my family asked me about my day, I said it was fine. I might have learned something if I had told them the truth: the work was too hard, but after the first morning I could bear it. And all summer it would be hard; after we finished the foundation, I would be transferred to another crew. We would build a mess hall at a Boy Scout camp and, with a black man, I would dig a septic tank in clay so hard that the foreman kept hosing water into it as we dug; black men and I would push wheelbarrows of mixed cement; on my shoulder I would carry eighty-pound bags of dry cement, twenty-five pounds less than my own weight; and at the summer's end, my body would be twenty pounds heavier. If I had told these three people who loved me that I did not understand my weak body's stamina, they might have taught me why something terrible had so quickly changed to something arduous.

It is time to thank my father for wanting me to work and telling me I had to work and getting the job for me and buying me lunch and a pith helmet instead of taking me home to my mother and sister. He may have wanted to take me home. But he knew he must not, and he came tenderly to me. My mother would have been at home that afternoon; if he had taken me to her, she would have given me iced tea and, after my shower, a hot dinner. When my sister came home from work, she would have understood, and told me not to despise myself because I could not work with a pickax and a shovel. And I would have spent the summer at home, nestled in the love of the two women, peering at my father's face, and yearning to be someone I respected, a varsity second baseman, a halfback, someone cheerleaders and drum majorettes and pretty scholars loved; yearning to be a man among men, and that is where my father sent me with a helmet on my head.

Imperiled Men

H E WAS A NAVY PILOT IN WORLD WAR II
and in Korea and, when I knew him in 1961
for a few months before he killed himself, he was
the commander of the Air Group aboard an aircraft carrier, and we called him by the acronym
CAG. He shot himself with his thirty-eight-caliber
revolver because two investigators from the Office
of Naval Intelligence came aboard ship while we
were anchored off Iwakuni in Japan, and gave
the ship's captain a written report of their investigation of some of CAG's erotic life. CAG held
the rank of commander then; he was a much-
decorated combat pilot, and his duty as CAG was

one of great responsibility. The ship's executive officer, also a commander, summoned CAG to his office, where the two investigators were, and told him that his choices were to face a general court-martial or resign from the Navy. Less than half an hour later, CAG was dead in his stateroom. His body was flown to the United States; we were told that he did not have a family, and I do not know where he was buried. There was a memorial service aboard ship, but I do not remember it; I only remember a general sadness like mist in the passageways.

I did not really know him. I was a first lieutenant with the Marine Detachment; we guarded the planes' nuclear weapons stored belowdecks, ran the brig, and manned one of the antiaircraft gun mounts. We were fifty or so enlisted men and two officers among a ship's crew of thirty-five hundred officers and men. The Air Group was not included in the ship's company. They came aboard with their planes for our seven-month deployment in the western Pacific. I do not remember the number of pilots and bombardier-navigators, mechanics and flight controllers, and men who worked on the flight deck, but there were plenty of all, and day and night you could hear planes catapulting off the front of the deck and landing on its rear.

The flight deck was a thousand feet long, the ship weighed seventy thousand tons, and I rarely felt its motion. I came aboard in May for a year of duty and in August we left our port in San Francisco Bay and headed for Japan. One night on the voyage across, I sat in the wardroom drinking coffee with a lieutenant commander. The long tables were covered with white linen; the wardroom was open all night because men were always working. The lieutenant commander told me that Russian submarines tracked us, they recorded the sound of our propellers and could not be fooled by the sound of a decoy ship's propellers, they came even into San Francisco Bay to do this; and our submarines did the same with Russian carriers. He said that every time we tried in training exercises to evade our own submarines, we could not do it, and our destroyers could not track and stop them. He said: "So if the whistle blows, we'll get a nuclear fish up our ass, in the first thirty minutes. Our job is to get the birds in the air before that. They're going to Moscow."

"Where will they land afterward?"

"They won't. They know that."

The voyage to Japan was five or six weeks long because we did not go directly to Japan; the pilots flew air operations. Combat units are always training for war; but these men who flew in planes, and the men in orange suits and ear protectors who worked on the flight deck during landings and takeoffs, were engaging in something not at all as playful as Marine field exercises generally were. They were imperiled. One pilot told me that, from his fighter-bomber in the sky, the flight deck looked like an aspirin tablet. On the passage to

Japan, I became friendly with some pilots, drinking coffee in the wardroom, and I knew what CAG looked like because he was CAG. He had dark skin and alert eyes, and he walked proudly. Then in Japan, I sometimes drank with young pilots. I was a robust twenty-five-year-old, one of two Marine officers aboard ship, and I did not want to be outdone at anything by anyone. But I could not stay with the pilots; I had to leave them in the bar, drinking and talking and laughing, and make my way back to the ship and sleep and wake with a hangover. Next day, the pilots flew; if we did not go to sea, they flew from a base on land. Once I asked one of them how he did it.

"The pure oxygen. Soon as you put on the mask, your head clears."

It was not simply the oxygen, and I did not understand any of these wild, brave, and very efficient men until years later when I read Tom Wolfe's *The Right Stuff*.

Months after CAG was dead, I saw another pilot die. I worked belowdecks with the Marine Detachment, but that warm gray afternoon the entire ship was in a simulated condition of war, and my part was to stand four hours of watch in a small turret high above the ship. I could move the turret in a circular way by pressing a button, and I looked through binoculars for planes or ships in the hundred-and-eighty-degree arc of our port side. On the flight deck, planes were taking off. Two parallel catapults launched planes straight off the front of the ship, and quickly they rose and climbed. A third and fourth catapult were on the port side where the flight deck angled sharply out to the left, short of the bow. From my turret, I looked down at the ship's bridge and the flight deck. A helicopter flew low near the ship, and planes were taking off. On the deck were men in orange suits and ear protectors; on both sides of the ship, just beneath the flight deck, were nets for these men to jump into, to save themselves from being killed by a landing plane that veered or skidded or crashed. One night, I inspected a Marine guarding a plane on the flight deck; we had a sentry there because the plane carried a nuclear bomb. I stepped from a hatch into the absolute darkness of a night at sea, and into a strong wind that lifted my body with each step. I was afraid it would lift me off the deck and hurl me into the sea, where I would tread water in that great expanse and depth while the ship went on its way; tomorrow they would learn that I was missing. I found the plane and the Marine; he stood with one arm around the cable that held the wing to the deck.

In the turret, I was facing aft when it happened: men in orange were at the rear of the flight deck; then they sprinted forward and I moved my turret toward the bow and saw a plane in the gray sea, and an orange-suited pilot lying facedown in the water, his parachute floating beyond his head, moving toward the rear of the ship. The plane had dropped off that third catapult and now water covered its wing, then its cockpit, and it sank. The pilot was behind the ship; his limbs did not move, his face was in the sea, and his parachute was filling with water and starting to sink. The helicopter hovered low and a sailor on a rope descended from it; he wore orange, and I watched him coming down and the pilot floating and the parachute sinking beneath the waves. There was still some length of parachute line remaining when the sailor reached the pilot; he grabbed him; then the parachute lines tightened their pull and drew the pilot down. There was only the sea now beneath the sailor on the rope. Then he ascended.

I shared a stateroom with a Navy lieutenant, an officer of medical administration, a very tall and strong man from Oklahoma. He had been an enlisted man, had once been a corpsman aboard a submarine operating off the coast of Russia, and one night their periscope was spotted, destroyers came after them, and they dived and sat at the bottom and listened by sonar to the destroyers' sonar trying to find them. He told me about the sailor who tried to save the pilot. In the dispensary, they gave him brandy, and the sailor wept and said he was trained to do that job, and this was his first time, and he had failed. Of course he had not failed. No man could lift another man attached to a parachute filled with water. Some people said the helicopter had not stayed close enough to the ship while planes were taking off. Some said the pilot was probably already dead; his plane dropped from the ship, and he ejected himself high into the air, but not high enough for his parachute to ease his fall. This was all talk about the mathematics of violent death; the pilot was killed because he flew airplanes from a ship at sea.

He was a lieutenant commander and I knew his face and name. As he was being catapulted, his landing gear on the left side broke off and his plane skidded into the sea. He was married; his widow had been married before, also to a pilot who was killed in a crash. I wondered if it was her bad luck to meet only men who flew; years later, I believed that whatever in their spirits made these men fly also drew her to them.

I first spoke to CAG at the officers' club at the Navy base in Yokosuka. The officers of the Air Group hosted a party for the officers of the ship's company. We wore civilian suits and ties and gathered at the club to drink. There were no women. The party was a matter of protocol, probably a tradition among pilots and the officers of carriers; for us young officers, it meant getting happily drunk. I was doing this with pilots at the bar when one of them said: "Let's throw CAG into the pond."

He grinned at me as I looked to my left at the small shallow pond with pretty fish in it; then I looked past the pond at CAG, sitting on a soft leather chair, a drink in his hand, talking quietly with two or three other commanders sitting in soft leather chairs. All the pilots with me were grinning and saying yes, and the image of us lifting CAG from his chair and dropping him into the water gave me joy, and I put my drink on the bar and said: "Let's *go*."

I ran across the room to CAG, grabbed the lapels of his coat, jerked him up from his chair, and saw his drink spill onto his suit; then I fell backward to the floor, still holding his lapels, and pulled him down on top of me. There was no one else with me. He was not angry yet, but I was a frightened fool. I released his lapels and turned my head and looked back at the laughing pilots. Out of my vision, the party was loud, hundreds of drinking officers who had not seen this, and CAG sounded only puzzled when he said: "What's going on?"

He stood and brushed at the drink on his suit, watching me get up from the floor. I stood not quite at attention but not at ease either. I said: "Sir, I'm Marine Lieutenant Dubus. Your pilots fooled me." I nodded toward them at the bar. CAG smiled. "They said: 'Let's throw CAG into the pond.' But, sir, the joke was on me."

He was still smiling.

"I'm very sorry, sir."

"That's all right, Lieutenant."

"Can I get the Commander another drink, sir?"

"Sure," he said, and told me what he was drinking, and I got it from the bar, where the pilots were red-faced and happy, and took it to CAG, who was sitting in the chair again, along with the other commanders. He smiled and thanked me, and the commanders smiled; then I returned to the young pilots and we all laughed.

Until a few months later, on the day he killed himself, the only words I spoke to CAG were greetings. One night, I saw him sitting with a woman in the officers' club, and I wished him good evening. A few times, I saw him in the ship's passageways; I recognized him seconds before the features of his face were clear: he had a graceful, athletic stride that dipped his shoulders. I saluted and said good morning, sir, or good afternoon, sir. He smiled as he returned my salute and greeting, his eyes and voice mirthful, and I knew that he was seeing me again pulling him out of his chair and down to the floor, then standing to explain myself and apologize. I liked being a memory that gave him sudden and passing amusement.

On a warm sunlit day, we were anchored off Iwakuni, and I planned to go with other crew members on a bus to Hiroshima. I put on civilian clothes and went down the ladder to the boat that would take us ashore. I was not happily going to Hiroshima; I was going because I am an American, and I felt that I should look at it, and be in it. I found a seat on the rocking boat, then saw CAG in civilian clothes coming down the ladder. There were few seats remaining, and he chose the one next to me. He asked me where I was going, then said he was going to Hiroshima too. I was relieved and grateful; while CAG was flying planes in World War II, I was a boy buying saving stamps and taking scrap metal to school. On the bus, he would talk to me about war, and in Hiroshima I would walk with him, and look with him, and his seasoned steps and eyes would steady mine. Then from the ship above us the officer of the deck called down: "CAG?"

CAG turned and looked up at him, a lieutenant junior grade in white cap and short-sleeved shirt and trousers.

"Sir, the executive officer would like to see you."

I do not remember what CAG said to me. I only remember my disappointment when he told the boat's officer to go ashore without him. All I saw in CAG's face was the look of a man called from rest back to his job. He climbed the ladder, and soon the boat pulled away.

Perhaps when I reached Hiroshima, CAG was dead; I do not remember the ruins at ground zero, or what I saw in the museum. I walked and looked, and stood for a long time at a low arch with an open space at the ground, and in that space was a stone box that held the names of all who had died on the day of the bombing, and all who had died since because of the bomb. That night, I ate dinner ashore, then rode the boat to the ship, went to my empty room, climbed to my upper bunk, and slept for only a while, till the quiet voice of my roommate woke me: "The body will be flown to Okinawa."

I looked at him standing at his desk and speaking into the telephone.

"Yes. A thirty-eight in the temple. Yes."

I turned on my reading lamp and watched him put the phone down. He was sad, and he looked at me. I said: "Did someone commit suicide?"

"CAG."

"CAG?"

I sat up.

"The ONI investigated him."

Then I knew what I had not known I knew, and I said: "Was he a homosexual?"

"Yes."

He told me two investigators from the Office of Naval Intelligence had come aboard that morning and had given the captain their report. The investigators were with the executive officer when he summoned CAG to his office and showed him the report and told him that he could either resign or face a general court-martial. Then CAG went to his room. Fifteen minutes later, the executive officer phoned him; when he did not answer, the executive officer and the investigators ran to his room. He was on his bunk, shot in the right temple, his revolver in his hand. His eyelids fluttered; he was unconscious but still alive, and he died from bleeding.

"They *ran*?" I said. "They *ran* to his room?"

Ten years later, one of my shipmates came to visit me in Massachusetts; we had been civilians for a long time. In my kitchen, we were drinking beer, and he said: "I couldn't tell you this aboard ship, because I worked in the legal office. They called CAG back from that boat you were on, because he knew the ONI was aboard. His plane was on the ground in Iwakuni. They were afraid he was going to fly it and crash into the sea and they'd lose the plane."

All thirty-five hundred men of the ship's crew did not mourn. Not every one of the hundreds of men in the Air Group mourned. But the shock was general and hundreds of men did mourn, and each morning we woke to it, and it was in our talk in the wardroom and in the passageways. In the closed air of the ship, it touched us, and it lived above us on the flight deck, and in the sky. One night at sea, a young pilot came to my room; his face was sunburned and sad. We sat in desk chairs, and he said: "The morale is very bad now. The whole Group. It's just shot."

"Did y'all know about him?"

"We all knew. We didn't care. We would have followed him into hell."

Yes: they would have followed him, diving in tunnels to the flaming center of the earth. When he was their leader, they were ready every day and every night to fly with him from a doomed ship, and follow him to Moscow, to perish in their brilliant passion.

A Hemingway Story

IN MY THIRTIETH SUMMER, IN 1966, I
read many stories by John O'Hara, and read
Hemingway's stories again, and his "In Another
Country" challenged me more than I could know
then. That summer was my last at the University of
Iowa; I had a master of fine arts degree and, beginning in the fall, a job as a teacher, in Massachusetts.
My wife and four children and I would move there
in August. Until then, we lived in Iowa City and I
taught two freshman rhetoric classes four mornings a week, then went home to eat lunch and
write. I wrote in my den at the front of the house, a
small room with large windows, and I looked out
across the lawn at an intersection of streets shaded

by tall trees. I was trying to learn to write stories, and was reading O'Hara and Hemingway as a carpenter might look at an excellent house someone else has built.

"In Another Country" became that summer one of my favorite stories written by anyone, and it still is. But I could not fully understand the story. "What's it *about*?" I said to a friend as we drove in his car to the university track to run laps. He said: "It's about the futility of cures." That nestled beneath my heart, displaced my confusion. Yes. The futility of cures. Then everything connected and formed a whole, and in the car with my friend, then running with him around the track, I saw the story as you see a painting, and one of the central images was the black silk handkerchief covering the wound where the young man's nose had been.

Kurt Vonnegut was our neighbor. We had adjacent lawns; he lived behind us, at the top of the hill. One day that summer, he was outside on his lawn or on his front porch four times when I was outside, and we waved and called to each other. The first time, I was walking home from teaching, wearing slacks and a shirt; the next time, I was wearing shorts and a T-shirt I had put on to write; then I wore gym shorts without a shirt and drove to the track; in late afternoon, wearing another pair of slacks and another shirt, I walked up to his house to drink. He was sitting on his front porch and, as I approached, he said: "Andre, you change clothes more than a Barbie doll."

Kurt did not have a telephone. That summer, the English department hosted a conference, and one afternoon a man from the department called me and asked me to ask Kurt to meet Ralph Ellison at the airport later in the day, then Mrs. Ellison at the train. She did not like to fly. I went up to Kurt's house, and he came to the back door. I said: "They want us to pick up Ellison at the airport. Then his wife at the train."

"Swell. I'll drive."

Later, he came driving down the brick road from his house and I got in the car and saw a paperback of *Invisible Man* between us on the seat. The airport was in Cedar Rapids, a short drive. I said: "Are you going to leave the book there?"

"I'm teaching it. I thought it'd be phony to take it out of the car."

It was a hot afternoon. We left town and were on the highway, the corn was tall and green under the huge midwestern sky, and I said: "They didn't really ask for both of us to pick up Ellison. Just you."

"I knew that."

"Thanks. How are we going to recognize him? Do we just walk up to the only Negro who gets off the plane?"

Kurt looked at me and said: "Shit."

"We could just walk past him, pretend we couldn't see him."

"That's so good, we ought to do it."

The terminal was small and we stood outside

and watched the plane land, and the people filing out of it, and there was one black man. We went to him and Kurt said: "Ralph Ellison?" and Ellison smiled and said: "Yes," and we shook his hand and got his things and went to the car. I sat in back, and watched Ellison. He saw *Invisible Man* at once but did not say anything. As we rode on the highway, he looked at the cornfields and talked fondly of the times he had hunted pheasants here with Vance Bourjaily. Then he picked up his book and said: "It's still around."

Kurt told him he was teaching it, and I must have told him I loved it, because I did and I do, but I only remember watching him and listening to him. Kurt asked him if he wanted a drink. He did. We went to a bar near the university, and sat in a booth, Ellison opposite Kurt and me, and ordered vodka martinis. We talked about jazz and books, and Ellison said that before starting *Invisible Man* he had read Malraux's *Man's Fate* forty times. He liked the combination of melodrama and philosophy, he said, and he liked that in Dostoyevski too. We ordered martinis again and I was no longer shy. I looked at Ellison's eyes and said: "I've been rereading Hemingway's stories this summer, and I think my favorite is 'In Another Country.' "

He looked moved by remembrance, as he had in the car, talking about hunting with Vance. Looking at us, he recited the story's first paragraph: " 'In the fall the war was always there, but we did not go to it any more. It was cold in the fall in Milan and the dark came very early. Then the electric lights came on, and it was pleasant along the streets looking in the windows. There was much game hanging outside the shops, and the snow powdered in the fur of the foxes and the wind blew their tails. The deer hung stiff and heavy and empty, and small birds blew in the wind and the wind turned their feathers. It was a cold fall and the wind came down from the mountains.' "

When we took Ellison to his room on the campus, it was time for us to go to the train station and meet his wife. Kurt said to Ellison: "How will we recognize her?"

"She's wearing a gray dress and carrying a beige raincoat." He smiled. "And she's colored."

Wanting to know absolutely what a story is about, and to be able to say it in a few sentences, is dangerous: it can lead us to wanting to possess a story as we possess a cup. We know the function of a cup, and we drink from it, wash it, put it on a shelf, and it remains a thing we own and control, unless it slips from our hands into the control of gravity; or unless someone else breaks it, or uses it to give us poisoned tea. A story can always break into pieces while it sits inside a book on a shelf; and, decades after we have read it even twenty times, it can open us up, by cut or caress, to a new truth.

I taught at Bradford College in Massachusetts

for eighteen years, and in my first year, and many times afterward, I assigned "In Another Country" to students. The first time I talked about it in a classroom, I understood more of it, because of what the students said, and also because of what I said: words that I did not know I would say, giving voice to ideas I did not know I had, and to images I had not seen in my mind. I began by telling them the story was about the futility of cures; by the end of the class, I knew it was not. Through my years of teaching, I learned to walk into a classroom wondering what I would say, rather than knowing what I would say. Then I learned by hearing myself speak; the source of my speaking was our mysterious harmony with truths we know, though very often our knowledge of them is hidden from us. Now, as a retired teacher, I mistrust all prepared statements by anyone, and by me.

Still, after discussing "In Another Country" the first time with Bradford students, I did go into the classroom, in the years after that, knowing exactly what I would say about the story. Probably ten times in those eighteen years, I assigned "In Another Country" and began our discussion by focusing on the images in the first two paragraphs, the narrator—who may be Nick Adams—bringing us to the hospital, and to the machines "that were to make so much difference," and I talked about the tone of that phrase, a tone achieved by the music of the two paragraphs, a tone that tells us the machines will make nothing different.

The story shifts then to the Italian major. He was a champion fencer before the war; now he is a wounded man whose right hand is shrunken; it is the size of a baby's hand, and he puts it into a machine that the doctor says will restore it to its normal size. Neither the major's hand nor the major will ever be normal. The narrator's knee is injured and the small proportion he gives it in the story lets us know that it will be healed. I told my students, when they were trying to understand a story that seemed difficult, to look at its proportion: the physical space a writer gives each element of the story. "In Another Country" moves swiftly from the futility of cures, to what it is that the physical curing cannot touch; and, yes, the young man who lost his nose and covered his face with a black silk handkerchief is a thematic image in the story, but it is not in the center of the picture, it is off to the side.

In the center of this canvas is death. That is why the narrator, though his knee will be normal again, will not himself be normal. Or perhaps not for a very long time. After the first hospital scene, he tells us of his other comrades, the Italian soldiers he walks home from the hospital with; all of them, in the war, have lived with death. Because of this, they feel detached, and they feel insulated from civilians and others who have not been in the war. The narrator is frightened, and at night he moves from the light of one streetlamp to another. He does not want to go to the war again. So the story now has moved from the futility of cures back to war, where it began with its opening line and the paragraph that shows us lovely pictures of Milan; while, beneath that tactile beauty, the music is the sound of something lost, and the loss of it has changed even the sound of the wind, and the sight of blowing snow on the fur of animals.

A war story, then; and while the major and narrator sit at their machines in the hospital, the major teaches Italian grammar to the narrator. I cannot know why Hemingway chose Italian grammar, but my deepest guess is that his choice was perfect: two wounded men, talking about language, rather than faith in the machines, hope for healing, or the horror of war. I am not saying they ought to be speaking about these things. There are times when it is best to be quiet, to endure, to wait. Hemingway may be our writer who has been the most badly read. His characters are as afraid of pain and death as anyone else. They feel it, they think about it, and they talk about it with people they love. With the Italian major, the narrator talks about grammar.

Then the story moves again, in the final scene. Until now, it has seemed to be a story about young men who have lost that joy in being alive that is normal for young and healthy people, who have not yet learned that within the hour they may be dead. The story has been about that spiritual aging that war can cause: in a few moments, a young soldier can see and hear enough, taste and touch and smell enough, to age his spirit by decades, while his body has not aged at all. The quickness of this change, of the spirit's immersion in horror, may cause a state of detachment from people whose lives are still normal, and who receive mortality's potion, drop by tiny drop, not in a torrent.

But in the story's final scene, the major furiously and bitterly grieves, scolds the narrator, then apologizes, says that his wife has just died, and, crying, leaves the room where the machines are. From their doctor, the narrator learns that the major had waited to marry until he was out of the war. His wife contracted pneumonia and in a few days she was dead, and now in the story, death is no longer the haunting demon of soldiers who have looked into its eyes. It is what no one can escape. The major reasonably believed he was the one in danger, until he was home from the war. Then death attacked his exposed flank, and breathed pneumonia into his wife. The story has completed its movement. A few notes remain: softly, a piano and bass, and faint drums and cymbals; we see the major returning to put his hand in the machine. He keeps doing this.

Two years after I retired from teaching, and twenty years after that last summer in Iowa City, I was crippled in an instant when a car hit me, and I was in a hospital for nearly two months. I suffered with pain, and I thought very often of Ernest Hemingway, and how much physical pain he had suffered, and how well he had written about it. In the hospital, I did not think about "In Another Country." I thought about "The Gambler, the Nun, and the Radio," and was both enlightened and amused, for always when I had talked about that story with students, I had moved quickly past the physical pain and focused on the metaphysical. Philosophy is abundant in that story; but I had to live in pain, on a hospital bed, before I could see that bodily pain deserved much more than I had given it. Always I had spent one fifty-minute class on the story. I should have used two class sessions; the first one would have been about pain.

A year after my injury, in a time of spiritual pain, I dreamed one night that I was standing on both my legs with other people in a brightly lit kitchen near the end of the day. I did not recognize any of the people, but in the dream they were my friends; one was a woman who was deeply hurting me. We were all standing, and I was pretending to be happy, and no one could see my pain. I stood near the stove. The kitchen door to the lawn was open, and there was a screen door, and, from outside, Ernest Hemingway opened it and walked in, looking at me across the length of the room. He wore his fishing cap with a long visor. He walked straight to me and said: "Let's go fishing." I walked with him, outside and down a sloping lawn to a wharf. We went to the end of the wharf, where a large boat

with an inboard motor was tied. Then we stood in
the cabin, Hemingway at my right and holding the
wheel with both hands; we moved on a calm bay,
and were going out to sea. It was dusk and I wondered if it was too late to go to sea, and I had not
seen him carrying fishing rods, and I wondered if
he had forgotten them. But I worried for only a
moment. Then I looked up at his profile and knew
that he knew what he was doing. He had a mus-
tache but no beard and was about forty and still
handsome.

The next night, a writers' workshop I host gathered in my living room. When they left, I sat in my
wheelchair in the dining room and remembered
my dream, and remarked for the first time that
Hemingway had his head, and I had my missing
leg, and the leg I do have was no longer damaged.
Then I remembered reading something that John
Cheever either wrote or said: during one long dark
night of the soul, Ernest Hemingway spoke to him.
Cheever said that he had never heard Hemingway's voice, but he knew that this was his voice,
telling Cheever that his present pain was only the
beginning. Then, sitting in my chair in the quiet
night, I believed that Hemingway had come to me
while I was suffering, and had taken me away from
it, out to sea, where we could fish.

A few months later, in winter, I wrote to Father
Bruce Ritter at Covenant House in New York and
told him that I was crippled and had not yet

learned to drive with hand controls; that my young daughters were no longer living with me; that I hosted, without pay, a writers' workshop, but its members could afford to pay anyone for what I did, and they did not really need me; and that I felt that when I was not with my children, I was no longer a useful part of the world. Father Ritter wrote to me, suggesting that I tutor a couple of high school students. In Haverhill, there is a home for girls between the ages of fourteen and eighteen. They are in protective custody of the state, because of what people have done to them. In summer, I phoned the home and asked if they wanted a volunteer. Someone drove me there to meet the man in charge of education. A light rain was falling. At the home, I looked through the car window at a second-story window and saw an old and long-soiled toy, a stuffed dog. The man came out and stood in the rain and I asked him what I could do. He said: "Give them stories about real people. Give them words and images. They're afraid of those."

So that fall, in 1988, we began; and nearly eight years later, girls with a staff woman still come to my house on Monday nights, and we read. For the first seven years, I read to them; then they told me they wanted to read, and now I simply choose a book, provide soft drinks and ashtrays, and listen. One night in the fall of 1991, five years after my injury, I read "In Another Country" to a few girls and a staff woman. This was the first time I had read it since my crippling. I planned to read it to the girls, then say about it what I had said so many times to students at Bradford College. I stopped often while reading the story, to tell them about images and thematic shifts. When I finished reading it, I talked about each part of it again, building to my explanation of the story's closing lines: "The major did not come to the hospital for three days. Then he came at the usual hour, wearing a black band on the sleeve of his uniform. When he came back, there were large framed photographs around the wall, of all sorts of wounds before and after they had been cured by the machines. In front of the machine the major used were three photographs of hands like his that were completely restored. I do not know where the doctor got them. I always understood we were the first to use the machines. The photographs did not make much difference to the major because he only looked out the window."

Then, because of my own five years of agony, of sleeping at night and in my dreams walking on two legs, then waking each morning to being crippled, of praying and willing myself out of bed to confront the day, of having to learn a new way to live after living nearly fifty years with a whole body— then, because of all this, I saw something I had never seen in the story, and I do not know whether Hemingway saw it when he wrote it or later or never, but there it was, there it is, and with passion and joy I looked up from the book, looked at the girls' faces, and said: "This story is about healing too. The major keeps going to the machines. And he doesn't believe in them. But he gets out of his bed in the morning. He brushes his teeth. He shaves. He combs his hair. He puts on his uniform. He leaves the place where he lives. He walks to the hospital, and sits at the machines. Every one of those actions is a movement away from suicide. Away from despair. Look at him. Three days after his wife has died, he is in motion. He is sad. He will not get over this. And he will get over this. His hand won't be cured, but someday he will meet another woman. And he will love her. Because he is alive."

The girls watched me, nodding their heads, those girls who had suffered and still suffered; but for now, on this Monday night, they sat on my couch, and happily watched me discover a truth; or watched a truth discover me, when I was ready for it.

Grace

OFTEN WE RECEIVE GRACE WITHOUT knowing it, and often we do not know it because when grace comes, we are already joyful or resilient or serene, or in another good state that grace brings. Sometimes we are impassioned. For five years, my first wife and I practiced the rhythm method of birth control. I was in the Marines then. We wanted several children and were trying to have them two years apart. They were born in August of 1958, September of 1959, November of 1960, and February of 1963.

Twice in those years, my wife and I made love when we knew she was ovulating. Once was on

Christmas Eve in 1958, while visiting her sister in Ohio, and she conceived our second child. The next time was in California, at Camp Pendleton, one morning before I went to work. We had been married less than two years, and our little girl and baby boy were sleeping, I was in uniform and waiting for the car pool of lieutenants, my wife was beautiful, and the calendar told us she was ovulating. Suddenly, still clothed save for our legs and loins, we were making love. She did not conceive. But we had to wait a long time to know that, or what then seemed a long time. Making love with her that morning, I knew fully who I was, where I was, what I was doing; and I felt that she and I, in each other's arms, were at the edge of the universe.

Years later, I felt this with another woman; but it had nothing to do with conception, and I was frightened and sad, for I was no longer with my wife. Yet my flesh remembered her, as my flesh now remembers walking; and, while the woman and I made love, I knew that as dear as she was to me, my flesh and spirit had gone too far, spun into space by the centrifugal force of my first love for my first wife. Motion from that spin has stayed with me, off and on, through the years. But on that morning in Southern California, surely grace flowed between us as we flung away certainty, and said yes to the unknown, out at the edge of light, where it ends, or becomes more brilliant.

Mailer at the Algonquin

O**N A GRAY THURSDAY MORNING IN LATE** winter or early spring of 1967, my editor phoned and summoned me and my wife to New York. He wanted us to fly there from Boston on Friday morning; we would have lunch at the Algonquin with the publisher and the house lawyer, and he would put us up at the Plaza. "The Plaza?" my wife said. "That's where Scott and Zelda stayed." Pat and I did not want to be like Scott and Zelda, but we did want a painless and durable piece of that glamour. My first book was coming out in the summer, I was thirty years old, and I knew the trip to New York was trouble, and that I would have to bring integrity there and come back home with it too.

But before I could turn my energy to that, I had two classes to teach Thursday afternoon, and we needed someone to stay with our four children; and, to go to New York, Pat needed clothes. I taught at Bradford Junior College, a two-year college for women in Haverhill, Massachusetts (later it became a four-year coeducational college), and the students were wealthy, or their parents were, and a small group of them had become friends of our family; often they spent weekends with us, to get away from the dormitory. We lived in a furnished two-hundred-year-old house just across the border in southern New Hampshire, built on seventy acres of wooded land with a meadow and a swimming pool. The landlord simply wanted someone to be in the house while he worked for a year or two in another state; our rent was a hundred dollars a month. That Thursday afternoon on the campus, I asked two of the students to help us, and after classes they came to our house for dinner, and they showed Pat a selection of clothes. She chose three outfits: one to wear on the plane and to lunch, one for dinner Friday night, one for Saturday morning's breakfast at the Plaza and the flight home. The students slept on couches downstairs and Pat and I went to bed upstairs, and I could not sleep.

In the Marines, I had a year of sea duty aboard

an aircraft carrier; I was a first lieutenant, the executive officer of the Marine Detachment. We had fifty-five enlisted men, and me and my captain. For a week or so, while my captain was in a Navy hospital in Japan, I was the acting commanding officer, and something happened, something whose elements were injustice, hypocrisy, and my first confrontation with a bureaucrat: a man who used a swivel chair and the passive voice, and precedents and rules and procedures, to turn away from the lonely complexity of the human heart.

For years, I told this story to friends. Then one night in Iowa City, where I was a graduate student after the Marines, a friend said: "That's a good story; you should write it as a novel." So I began. I am not a novelist, but I did not know it then. I started with a notebook, making up characters: a lieutenant, four young Marines, a first sergeant, a captain who would have to go to a hospital, two girlfriends, and so on, and let all of this gestate for months, then read Chekhov's *The Duel* again, to be immersed in plot, for *The Duel* is so clearly and beautifully built with a casual sequence of events. Then I went to work, and wrote *The Lieutenant* in two and a half months—a short story takes longer for me now—and sent it to Dial Press, because I had met the editor in chief when he came to Iowa for a publishers' conference. I liked him; he was a wonderful writer and he is an even better one now, and if I saw him more than once a decade, I know

I would love him. He took the novel in the winter of 1966, and at the end of that summer, Pat and I moved with our children to the big house, the pool, the seventy acres of woods and a meadow, and then winter or late spring came and the editor's call and the Thursday night when I lay awake, knowing that the next day I would look into the jaws of the wolf.

That winter, a friend of mine had published a novel, and one of his brothers had sued him, and the publisher had taken the novel out of the bookstores. So I knew, on that long Thursday night in New Hampshire, that tomorrow's lunch at the Algonquin was a meeting about the possibility of being sued, and that the lawyer, the publisher, and my editor would want me to change my novel. The people in my novel were not the people I had known aboard ship, but I had used their bodies, had given their bodies to the characters in my story. I often use bodies and faces I know, or composites of them, but I have never written fiction about anyone I know, even my parents, though I have written stories about my parents and me, have even written dialogue my parents actually spoke, and acts they performed; but on the page, they are only my parents in a sensate way, as I perceived them when I was a child, remembered them as a man, then looked at them through the prism and sometimes kaleidoscope of a story, so that finally on the page they are not themselves. I have never known anyone as deeply as I know a character who comes to me through the work of writing a story, because I have never been able to feel absolutely what another human being is feeling. The perception of a character in a story written with compassion is, for both the reader and the writer, a perception closer to divine than human. William Styron's Helen Loftis in *Lie Down in Darkness* is a woman who causes great pain, but Styron shows us her heart more clearly and fully than we are able to see the hearts of human beings we actually know, and most readers will feel compassion and love for Helen Loftis, although in her actions and words this woman is an awful burden on anyone who needs her love and wishes to love her in return. So I never believe that real people are in fiction, because if the writer is not compassionate, the character is distorted by the writer's pain or bitterness or mean spirit; and if the writer is compassionate, the writer will become one with the character, and the reader will too, and the character is a truly created one whose deepest elements are universal. In *The Lieutenant,* there are no real people; but some of them looked like people who indeed walked the decks of a real ship.

Then, lying in the dark, challenged and afraid, it came to me: tomorrow at lunch, they would ask me to write the novel again, to make the story occur on land rather than on a ship at sea. For a long time, I lay with that certainty. Then I had my answer to them: a lieutenant would not have as much responsibility on land as my lieutenant had at sea. On land, all the judicial elements of my story would be dealt with by a battalion commander. I was both relieved and strengthened, and I wanted the hours of night and morning ahead of me to be out of the way, as if they were a curtain I could raise, so at this moment I could be sitting at the table and hearing my editor ask me to move the novel from sea to land, so I could say no, and fly back home and lie in this bed with peace.

I turned on the bedside lamp. On the floor was Mailer: a paperback copy of *Advertisements for Myself.* I had not started reading it, but there it was, and I picked it up and read Mailer, who by then had endured every writer's peril I could imagine, including success, or what some people call success because that is what having a lot of readers and earning a lot of money look like; but success and failure come to a writer each day, a word or a sentence at a time. Mailer filled the room, the quiet house, my soul. In his book, he said not to give in to editors who want you to change your work, who say they are your friends, who say the changes will be good for you. He says it is better to be a good man than a good writer. That is how sleep came to me, with Mailer's encouraging voice.

Pat and I did not have enough cash for plane fare from Boston to New York and we did not have credit cards, and I do not know how Dial paid for our tickets; my editor assumed we were taking the shuttle and met us at whatever airport the shuttle flies to from Boston, but we flew on another plane, which landed at the other airport, so how were the tickets bought? It was early Friday afternoon, still cold and gray, and we waited a long time at the airport; then my editor came, and explained about the different flights and different airports. In the cab, he told us about New York's boroughs, and other things about New York, and I listened to this as you might listen to stories about a man who was going to meet you in an alley where he intended to beat you, and rob you, and then extort from you for the rest of your life. Pat knew this, and told the editor I did not care about New York, that I wanted to know what this lunch was about, but he said we'd get to that, and he pointed out the car windows and talked about New York, and I sat with my adrenaline and waited.

Perhaps this travel by cab from the airport to the Algonquin was the beginning and the sculpted end of my perception of New York; I did not see a river or the tops of buildings touching a wet gray sky; I saw only the fight ahead. I have been there many times since, and always have kept my eyes on the trail directly ahead of me, watching for predators. The people I've met who work in publishing have been stimulating and amusing company, and have been good people. But good people can sincerely want what is good for one, but not for the other. Publishing is, finally, a business, and this means a time will come when an editor must bring money into a conversation with a writer. Those of us who write would like this money simply to be a check with our names on it. Editors are very happy to arrange for such checks, but their job is also to earn money for the publishing house. This is not bad, of itself. It becomes bad when combined with other forces: when an editor's desire to make money for the house and for the writer is stronger than the editor's desire for the writer to make a good work of art—if in fact the editor is working with a writer who wants above all to make a good work of art.

One editor once suggested I add a forty-page section to a novella, *The Pretty Girl.* He said: "You'll make a lot of *mon*ey." He was, of course, not talking about my story anymore, except as a commodity that could be lengthened so it could be sold as a book. If it is your work the editor is talking about, and the editor is stimulating and amusing, your vanity can blossom and venality often sneaks up under the leaves and petals. Then you are in a condition of temptation. I write as a man who has had few dealings with New York publishing; I have some small stories of my own, and have heard longer and worse ones from friends. No dedicated celibate has been more wary in the presence of a woman on the hunt than I am when I go to that city, where enough money for a lifetime seems only a smile away, and where from the doors of hotels and apartments and cabs beautiful women appear like hope.

Mailer was at the Algonquin. I saw him as we walked in, Pat and my editor and I. In the night, he had been with me, and now he was eating lunch with a woman. We were passing him, he was on our right, and farther down the room, the publisher and house lawyer were waiting. I told my editor I wanted to meet Mailer. We went to his table, and as my editor spoke to him, Mailer stood, his eyes merry and intent. I extended my hand and as we shook, I said: "Mr. Mailer, I spent last night reading *Advertisements for Myself*, and I'm using it the way boxers use resin on the soles of their shoes before going into the ring; because I think these guys are going to try to screw me."

He grinned and his eyes brightened, and still shaking my hand, he said: "Well, that book's been used in a lot of ways, it may as well be used like this. Don't let them get to you."

Then we went to our table. I did not know then that you had to eat lunch first. When I asked them what we were there for, they said, "Oh, have a drink, let's eat, there's plenty of time." Einstein said that relativity is very simple: fifteen minutes is a long time if you are sitting on a hot stove, and a short time if a pretty woman is sitting on your lap. This lunch had begun for me nearly thirty hours ago. The waiter brought Bloody Marys; I was talking and moving my hands and I knocked over my full drink. This is more embarrassing when you are sober, because then you are clumsy instead of happy and drunk. But I was too poised for fighting to be too embarrassed, and the red juice on the white tablecloth and the waiter's cold eyes seemed small parts of the forces that had uprooted me and flown me here, away from my home and my desk, where my integrity as an artist had no enemy, no seductress, except the ones that existed in my own soul; and, since I made a living, though a scant one, by teaching, money was not one of the voices in my soul. At my desk, the only voices I had to ignore were not stimulating and amusing; they were dreary, frightened voices telling me to give up on a sentence, or a scene, or a story; and these are the voices a writer is born with, and a writer is born to ignore. Claire Bloom came into the Algonquin and sat at a table. To my left, Mailer was eating, and talking with the woman.

Then it was over, it was late afternoon, we were drinking coffee and smoking, and the editor and publisher and lawyer were talking about my friend's book and the lawsuit. Then my editor asked if mine could be changed, could be placed on land instead of at sea, and I told him calmly and briefly why it could not, and he agreed, they all agreed; and the lawyer said that in a suit the other side will list all similarities between the fictional characters and the plaintiffs, and I told them about my use of the bodies, and that I would change the color of their eyes and hair. Claire Bloom was gone, and Mailer was gone; we must have waved or nodded when he left, for all during lunch I watched him whenever I could. My editor said if we wanted to, we could go home with him on the train and meet his wife and stay with them for the night, and I knew Pat wanted to go to the Plaza, dine and make love and sleep there, wake and eat breakfast there. But I wanted now to drink with my editor and talk about books written by other people, and without a quarrel then or ever after, we did that, and we had a very good evening, the four of us, and next morning Pat and I flew home to our children and the two young women. We had hangovers and I had my integrity as a writer, but not as a husband, and for a long time now I have wished we had stayed at the Plaza, and I hope that Pat got there some night without me.

Brothers

I N THE WINTER OF 1974, I MET MY AGENT,
Philip Spitzer, and his brother, Michel. I had
liked Philip for months when he was only a voice
on the phone. I had sent him a collection of stories
in the summer of 1973, and he wanted to try to
sell it; till then, I had not had encouragement from
anyone in New York about a book of stories, without a novel. After that, I talked too often on the
phone with Philip. He was friendly and patient, but
I had no discipline then, and I phoned at least
every week to ask if a publisher had taken my book.
Of course if a publisher had taken it, Philip would
have called me. But I can be suddenly and power-

fully filled with a hope that feels like certainty: *an editor has just called Philip, now is the time, it is happening now*—something like that. In winter, he called to tell me he was going to visit his brother in Exeter, New Hampshire, and they would like to see me on their way north from the airport in Boston.

Philip is a sensitive man; calling me about having a drink together probably gave him some difficulty: he would know that, when I heard his voice, I would expect him to say he had sold my book. That happened later, in spring. I lived alone in a two-room apartment, up three flights of stairs Philip and Michel climbed one night. I had very little furniture, and one or two of us sat on the bed. Philip and Michel are witty, athletic, good-hearted men who like to tell jokes and stories. That evening, we became friends. It is a deep friendship, though we rarely see one another. I feel like a brother to them; a few summers ago, I went to the wedding of Michel's son, and either Philip or Michel pushed me up a sloping lawn to pose with the Spitzers for the family photograph; Michel's son said: "You're an honorary Spitzer."

In April, after meeting that winter, we went to the Boston Red Sox opening day at Fenway Park. I was a teacher then; I taught five afternoons a week, and had never been to opening day. But that year—and for the next twelve years, till I retired, early and burned-out—I canceled my classes and went to the game with Philip and Michel and my friend Jim Valhouli, a teacher of literature who twenty-one winters later broke through ice while skating on the Exeter River and drowned. Yet there we were, the four of us, in our thirties, laughing in Michel's car, on a holiday not only from work but from Time and what we perceived as our daily lives, and from what would become of us. That is what a baseball game gives. When Sandy Koufax retired from the Dodgers, he said that baseball was not reality; it entertained people and allowed them to escape for a few hours.

At a baseball game in Fenway Park, I feel like a boy, watching grown men on a playing field, and watching grown men and women in their seats in boxes and the grandstand, and faceless bodies across the field in the bleachers; watching them watch, cheer, eat, talk, drink; watching them go up and down the steps, for food, drinks, or the rest rooms. The sound of the crowd is steady, the calls of roaming vendors rising higher, as the cries of certain people do, those who yell at umpires, players, managers, and those who call to the players: *Good eye; You can do it,* as if they—we; I do it—had been infielders years ago, when the voices of infielders were part of the game, calling to the pitcher: *Come babe, come boy,* we used to say in spirited voices, our bodies poised, our weight on our toes, our gloves ready. During ball games at Fenway Park, strangers talk to one another about the game; people cheer when one catches a foul ball; vendors standing on steps hear an order from someone sitting in the middle of the row; the buyer hands money to someone in the next seat, who passes it on; the paper and coins move from hand to hand to the vendor, who places in these hands popcorn, hot dogs, peanuts, beer, soft drinks. Sometimes at Mass, I think of Fenway Park, for at Mass there is the same feeling of goodwill: people are there because they want to be, and I feel among friends who share a passion.

For me, baseball is real in a deeper way than much of what I do. I do not begin a baseball season hoping the Red Sox win a pennant and the World Series. I enjoy each game. Next day, I wait with excitement for the game on television that night or afternoon. Then I watch what happens and does not happen in a moment. I rarely concentrate on a moment of anything but writing and exercise and receiving Communion. Yet watching a game, I do. A batter steps out of the box, looks to his left at the third-base coach; the coach moves his hands, touches his arm, his chest, his face, his cap; the batter steps to the plate; the catcher's right fingers signal to the pitcher; the pitcher shakes his head; a runner on second creeps away from the base, glancing at the shortstop and second baseman; the catcher signals again, the pitcher nods, brings up his hands, kicks, throws. I watch the ball, and the batter. The ball is moving ninety-three miles an hour, but there is time for me to focus on it, maybe hold my breath, enough time so that it feels like waiting; then I am amazed: the batter not only hits the ball but times his swing so well that he pulls it, a line drive right of the third baseman, who somehow has time to dive for it, but he does not touch it; he is lying on the ground, the ball hits the grass a hundred feet behind him, as the left fielder sprints toward it, to stop it before it bounces and rolls to the fence.

The reality I am watching is moments of grace and skill, gifts received by men who do not turn away from them, but work with them for the few years they are granted. One spring, the batter will not be able to hit a fastball, the pitcher will not be able to throw one; the gifts are gone, as if they existed independent of men, staying with one for a time, then moving on to another, a boy in the womb, and when he is in elementary school, you can already see that he has it.

A Zen archer does not try to hit the target. With intense concentration, he draws the bow and waits; the target releases the arrow, and draws it to itself. A few summers ago, during an all-star game, retired pitcher Steve Carlton visited the television broadcasting booth. One of the announcers asked him if hitters had ever intimidated him. He said he had ignored the hitters and played an advance game of catch with his catcher; it's an elevated form of pitching, he said. I have told this many times to young writers, and have also told them that Wade Boggs watching a pitch come to the plate, starting his stride and swing, probably does not know his own name, for his whole being is concentrating on that moving white ball. I could have said this about any good hitter, or fielder, or pitcher: men whose intense focus on a baseball burns their consciousness of the past and future into ashes blown quickly up and away from the field. This happens over and over in a game, and these moments are so pure, they may be sacred; and they are not ephemeral; they seem so, because they exist in Time; but so did my friend Jim Valhouli; a river took his life, but it did not take the life he lived.

After that first opening day, we went to every one for twelve more years, the four of us becoming a crowd of sometimes forty men and women, writers, editors, teachers, publishers, booksellers, husbands, wives, boyfriends, girlfriends. In late fall, when the Red Sox ticket office opened, I would drive to Boston and buy tickets: two for me, ten for the Spitzer brothers, some for my publisher, David Godine, and people who worked for him, and always we had rows of good seats behind third or first base, and everyone sent me checks for their tickets. Cold weather postponed one game, and always we wore coats, hats, gloves, scarves. I wore a Red Sox jacket and cap. There must have been days with warm sun, our coats on our laps. In my memory, I see them all as warm days, weather for throwing and hitting and catching a baseball, for sitting and watching a game. The last year we went was 1986, my last spring as a biped, and in the late fall of that year, I was in a hospital bed in my home, my right leg in a full cast that would be on it till June, my left leg amputated above the knee, and none of us bought tickets for opening day.

I was thin and weak and in pain and could do very little for myself. I could eat, but not much; talk, read a book, try to write, but I could not lift my four-year-old daughter, who weighed thirty-five pounds. In March, walking to the bathtub with crutches and an artificial leg, with two strong women, a physical therapist and a home health aide, I took my first shower since a car hit me in July of 1986. I wore loose-fitting gym shorts. When I reached the tub, I slowly turned my back to it and the shower bench I would sit on, and held a grab bar on the wall as the women took the crutches; they squatted, held my leg and the artificial one, gripped my arms at the shoulders; then, as I held my breath, they rose, pulling up my leg and the other one, and eased me onto the bench. Now I could release my breath. They pulled off the leg, and unrolled onto mine a rubber sheath like a condom that covered the cast, and we laughed. I closed the curtain, pulled off my shorts, handed them to a woman whose hand was in the water from the faucet; when it was very warm, she pushed the lever to divert it, and out of the shower nozzle it came, spraying my face, my hair, my chest, hot joy on my body, which for eight months had felt unclean, and I closed my eyes to it, lifted my face to it, then washed my body, my hair, and stayed a long time in the shower, with a window at my right. Out the window were poplars on the steep hill behind my house, a hill I had loved to climb; at its top, near the electrical fences of the dairy farmer whose hill rises from mine till it peaks and descends to the Merrimack River, I had hung two rope hammocks. Sitting on the shower bench, in the blessing of hot water, I believed I would climb that short hill again. It would only take time. Then my right knee would bend, the damaged muscles and nerves would be again and for all my life sound, and, wearing jeans and boots, I would climb that hill, with my golden retriever, and I would lie on a shaded and swinging hammock, and while the dog lay on the grass chewing a fallen branch, I would look up through the poplars at a summer sky. In 1987, I watched opening day on television, sitting on the couch I transferred to from my wheelchair while my wife held the leg I could not lift in its cast.

So the Spitzer brothers and I saw thirteen baseball games, forty hours or so, with twenty or thirty or forty other people, some of whom I saw only on opening day. Jim Valhouli did not go to all the games. He left the college where we taught, and moved to Exeter to teach at Phillips Exeter Academy. Probably in the third year, some of us began meeting for lunch before the game, at a Japanese restaurant someone discovered on Newbury Street: the chef performing on the grill at our table, while some of us drank hot sake. In 1977, eight of us sat at a table, the Spitzers married but without their wives; I was with mine, and our friends George and Tom were with theirs. A year later, the Spitzers and George and Tom and I sat in the same restaurant, smelling and eating shrimp, filet mignon, chicken and vegetables and rice, talking about baseball, checking our watches, timing our pleasure so we could walk to Fenway Park and see the first pitch of the game. George was talking, and then he stopped, chopsticks in hand; he blushed, looking at the rest of us, his mouth open. Then he said: "Last year, we were all married."

We stopped eating, looked at one another: we were all divorced. Then we laughed, not at the dismal pain of divorce, not at the loss of hope, of faith, of love that divorce is; we laughed because it was opening day and during the year since the last one we had each lost, each suffered, some less than others; as our wives had, but then they had moved strongly, it seemed, onto new courses; and here we were, perhaps with invisible limps and aches and longings, eating Japanese food with wooden sticks, sitting as if poised in Time, waiting for the excitement of being with over thirty thousand people and watching a game that does not employ a clock.

I do not remember any of the games, only moments, and the one I remember with most love was in the early eighties. I had a wife again. The weather was good. Probably we wore jackets, but the sky was blue, the sun warm, and the Red Sox won. I happily left the game, walking with my wife and Philip and Michel, and other friends, slowly with the talking crowd, down the steps and the ramp, to the paler light and coolness beneath the grandstands, the smells of steamed hot dogs, beer, hamburgers, tobacco smoke, a faint scent of urine from the rest rooms, and the smells of people, of their clothes, hair, skin, makeup, and that indefinable smell in a crowd, as if you are smelling the fact of being alive. We moved slowly still, with thousands of others going to the sidewalks and streets that would be filled with people who, for now, were happy.

We reached an exit and walked into the sun again. About ten yards ahead, I saw eight or so white teenagers beating three black ones who lay on their backs on the ground, their arms covering their bleeding faces. I ran to them, jerked collars, necks, shoulders; pulled and pushed white boys, and grabbed the black ones, pulled them as they stood; I pushed them against a car to protect their backs, then turned to face the white boys. I raised my fists. "Police!" I yelled. I was both afraid and sad. I said to the white boys: "It's opening *day*. It's opening *day*." That is all I said, between cries for police. The white boys edged toward me, their fists ready; the one closest to me lunged, feinted punches, and hissed through his teeth. Not one of these boys was bleeding. "It's opening *day*," I said, waiting for the attack that would hurt. Then I felt a touch on my right shoulder, and then one on my left, and I looked, and Philip stood on one side of me, Michel on the other, their fists raised, and we stood like that, our shoulders touching, with the three bleeding boys behind us, until my wife came with police officers, who dispersed the white boys, then looked at the black boys' cuts, and sent them on their way.

As we went on ours, to drinks and dinner, then to drive to our homes in the night. Jim Valhouli was not with us that day; he would have joined us in front of the boys. Michel would marry again; then, nearly a year after my crippling, Philip would, and a few months after that I would not have a wife. All of it happened in our lives: the love of wives that was good and still is, with the pain of its loss, outside of Time; the baseball games I cannot remember but which still exist not only because they are recorded but because of what men brought to them and received from them, on the field, in the dugouts and bull pens; and what women and children and men brought to them and received in Fenway Park and at home with a television set or a radio; what athletic and passionate Jim Valhouli and his wife and two sons gave and received till the ice broke; and on that April afternoon, lit by the sun, those moments of violence, injustice, fear, and love, when my two friends came to my sides and stood with me, waiting.

Good-bye
to
Richard Yates

Y OU PHONED THAT NIGHT WHEN YOU were writing "Oh, Joseph, I'm So Tired," and asked if Mary would really have a donkey and why were they going to Bethlehem anyway. I told you about the Annunciation, and you said: "Well, everybody knew they were going steady, didn't they?" I remember how much you laughed, how easy it was to make you laugh, how much of your laughter was at yourself. It's your mornings I imagine, Dick. You never complained to me about your body, so I imagine you waking to a room, a world, that seemed to have enough air for everyone but you, and gathering yourself, putting on those gentleman's clothes you wore, and bringing your great heart and your pure writer's conscience to the desk, the legal pad, the pencil. You just kept doing it, morning after morning, and you inspired me, you gave me courage, taking your morning stand against your flesh and circumstance, writing prose that was a blade, a flame, a cloud, a breath. So you rest, old friend. And about all those words you wrote in all your books on my shelf, I say as you used to about a book or story you loved: They're swell, Dick, they're really swell; it's a sweetheart of a life's work, it's a sweetheart.

Sacraments

A SACRAMENT IS PHYSICAL, AND WITHIN
it is God's love; as a sandwich is physical, and
nutritious and pleasurable, and within it is love, if
someone makes it for you and gives it to you with
love; even harried or tired or impatient love, but
with love's direction and concern, love's again and
again wavering and distorted focus on goodness;
then God's love too is in the sandwich. A sacrament is an outward sign of God's love, they taught
me when I was a boy, and in the Catholic church
there are seven. But, no, I say, for the church is
catholic, the world is catholic, and there are seven
times seventy sacraments, to infinity. Today I sit at

my desk in June in Massachusetts; a breeze from the southeast comes through the window behind me, touches me, and goes through the open glass door in front of me. The sky is blue, and cumulus clouds are motionless above green trees lit brightly by the sun shining in dry air. In humid air, the leaves would be darker, but now they are bright, and you can see lighted space between them, so that each leaf is distinct; and each leaf is receiving sacraments of light and air and water and earth. So am I, in the breeze on my skin, the air I breathe, the sky and earth and trees I look at.

Sacraments are myriad. It is good to be baptized, to confess and be reconciled, to receive Communion, to be confirmed, to be ordained a priest, to marry, or to be anointed with the sacrament of healing. But it is limiting to believe that sacraments occur only in churches, or when someone comes to us in a hospital or at home and anoints our brows and eyes and ears, our noses and lips, hearts and hands and feet. I try to receive Communion daily, and I never go to Mass day after day after day, because I cannot sleep when I want to, I take pills, and if the pills allow me to sleep before midnight, I usually can wake up at seven-thirty and do what I must to get to Mass. But I know that when I do not go to Mass, I am still receiving Communion, because I desire it; and because God is in me, as He is in the light, the earth, the leaf. I only have to lie on my bed, waking after Mass has already ended, and I am receiving sacraments with each breath, as I did while I slept; with each movement of my body as I exercise my lower abdomen to ease the pain in my back caused by sitting for fifteen hours: in my wheelchair, my car, and on my couch, before going to bed for the night; receiving sacraments as I perform crunches and leg lifts, then dress and make the bed while sitting on it. Being at Mass and receiving Communion give me joy and strength. Receiving Communion of desire on my bed does not, for I cannot feel joy with my brain alone. I need sacraments I can receive through my senses. I need God manifested as Christ, who ate and drank and shat and suffered, and laughed. So I can dance with Him as the leaf dances in the breeze under the sun.

Not remembering that we are always receiving sacraments is an isolation the leaves do not have to endure: they receive and give, and they are green. Not remembering this is an isolation only the human soul has to endure. But the isolation of a human soul may be the cause of not remembering this. Between isolation and harmony, there is not always a vast distance. Sometimes it is a distance that can be traversed in a moment, by choosing to focus on the essence of what is occurring, rather than on its exterior: its difficulty or beauty, its demands or joy, peace or grief, passion or humor. This is not a matter of courage or discipline or will; it is a receptive condition.

Because I am divorced, on Tuesdays I drive to my daughters' school, where they are in the seventh and second grades. I have them with me on other days, and some nights, but Tuesday is the school day. They do not like the food at their school, and the school does not allow them to bring food, so after classes they are hungry, and I bring them sandwiches, potato chips, Cokes, Reese's peanut butter cups. My kitchen is very small; if one person is standing in it, I cannot make a three-hundred-and-sixty-degree turn. When I roll into the kitchen to make the girls' sandwiches, if I remember to stop at the first set of drawers on my right, just inside the door, and get plastic bags and write *Cadence* on one and *Madeleine* on the other, then stop at the second set of drawers and get three knives for spreading mayonnaise and mustard and cutting the sandwiches in half, then turn sharply left and reach over the sink for the cutting board leaning upright behind the faucet, then put all these things on the counter to my right, beside the refrigerator, and bend forward and reach into the refrigerator for the meat and cheese and mustard and mayonnaise, and reach up into the freezer for bread, I can do all of this with one turn of the chair. This is a First World problem; I ought to be only grateful. Sometimes I remember this, and then I believe that most biped fathers in the world would exchange their legs for my wheelchair and house and food, medical insurance and my daughters' school.

Making sandwiches while sitting in a wheelchair
is not physically difficult. But it can be a spiritual
trial; the chair always makes me remember my legs,
and how I lived with them. I am beginning my
ninth year as a cripple, and have learned to try to
move slowly, with concentration, with precision,
with peace. Forgetting plastic bags in the first set of
drawers and having to turn the chair around to get
them is nothing. The memory of having legs that
held me upright at this counter and the image of
simply turning from the counter and stepping to
the drawer are the demons I must keep at bay, or I
will rage and grieve because of space, and time,
and this wheeled thing that has replaced my legs.
So I must try to know the spiritual essence of what
I am doing.

On Tuesdays when I make lunches for my girls, I
focus on this: the sandwiches are sacraments. Not
the miracle of transubstantiation, but certainly
parallel with it, moving in the same direction. If I
could give my children my body to eat, again and
again without losing it, my body like the loaves and
fishes going endlessly into mouths and stomachs, I
would do it. And each motion is a sacrament, this
holding of plastic bags, of knives, of bread, of cutting board, this pushing of the chair, this spreading
of mustard on bread, this trimming of liverwurst,
of ham. All sacraments, as putting the lunches into
a zippered book bag is, and going down my six
ramps to my car is. I drive on the highway, to the
girls' town, to their school, and this is not simply a

transition; it is my love moving by car from a place where my girls are not to a place where they are; even if I do not feel or acknowledge it, this is a sacrament. If I remember it, then I feel it too. Feeling it does not always mean that I am a happy man driving in traffic; it simply means that I know what I am doing in the presence of God.

If I were much wiser, and much more patient, and had much greater concentration, I could sit in silence in my chair, look out my windows at a green tree and the blue sky, and know that breathing is a gift; that a breath is sufficient for the moment; and that breathing air is breathing God.

You can receive and give sacraments with a telephone. In a very lonely time, two years after my crippling, I met a woman with dark skin and black hair and wit and verbal grace. We were together for an autumn afternoon, and I liked her, and that evening I sat on my couch with her, and held and kissed her. Then she drove three and a half hours north to her home in Vermont. I had a car then, with hand controls, but I had not learned to drive it; my soul was not ready for the tension and fear. I did not see the woman until five weeks later. I courted her by telephone, daily or nightly or both. She agreed to visit me and my family at Thanksgiving. On Halloween, I had a heart attack, and courted her with the bedside telephone in the hospital. Once after midnight, while I was talking to her, a nurse came into the room, smiled at me, and took the clipboard from the foot of the bed and wrote what she saw. Next morning, in my wheelchair, I read: *Twelve-fifteen. Patient alert and cheerful, talking on the phone.*

In the five weeks since that sunlit October day when I first saw her, I knew this woman through her voice. Then on Thanksgiving, she drove to a motel in the town where I live, and in early afternoon came to my house for dinner with my family: my first wife and our four grown children, and one daughter's boyfriend and one son's girlfriend, and my two young daughters. That night, when the family left, she stayed and made love to my crippled body, which did not feel crippled with her, save for some pain in my leg. Making love can be a sacrament, if our souls are as naked as our bodies, if our souls are in harmony with our bodies, and through our bodies are embracing each other in love and fear and trembling, knowing that this act could be the beginning of a third human being, if we are a man and a woman; knowing that the roots and trunk of death are within each of us, and that one of its branches may block or rupture an artery as we kiss. Surely this is a sacrament, as it may not be if we are with someone whose arms we would not want holding us as, suddenly, in passion, we died; someone whose death in our arms would pierce us not with grief but regret, fear, shame; someone who would not want to give life to that third person who is always present in lovemaking between fertile men and women. On the day after

Thanksgiving, she checked out of the motel and stayed with me until Monday, and I loved her; then she went home.

She came to me on other weekends, four to six weeks apart, and we loved each other daily by telephone. That winter, she moved to New York City. I still did not drive, and her apartment was not a place I could enter and be in with my wheelchair; it was very small, and so was the shared bathroom down the hall. I could not fly to her, because my right knee does not bend, so I have to sit on the first seat of an airplane, and that means a first-class ticket. Trains are inaccessible horrors for someone in a wheelchair: the aisles are too narrow. A weekend in New York, if I flew there and stayed in a hotel, would have cost over a thousand dollars, before we bought a drink or a meal. So she flew to Boston or rode on the train, and a friend drove me to meet her. I was a virtual shut-in who was in love. One day a week, my oldest son drove me to horseback-riding lessons; in the barn, he pushed me up a ramp to a platform level with the horse's back, and I mounted and rode, guarded from falling by my son and volunteer women who walked and jogged beside me. A driver of a wheelchair van came for me two mornings a week and took me to Mass and left, then came back and took me to physical therapy, then came back and took me home, where I lay on my bed and held the telephone and talked to the woman, sometimes more than once a day. With the telephone, she gave me sacraments I needed during that fall and winter when my body seemed to be my enemy. We were lovers for a year, and then we were not, and now our love remains and sharing our flesh is no longer essential.

On Christmas Eve, in that year when we were lovers, I was very sad and I called her. The Christmas tree was in the living room, tall and full, and from the kitchen doorway, where I held the telephone, I could see in the front windows the reflection of the tree and its ornaments and lights. My young daughters' stockings were hanging at the windows, but my girls were at their mother's house, and would wake there Christmas morning, and would come to me in the afternoon. I was a crippled father in an empty house. In my life, I have been too much a father in an empty house; and since the vocation of fatherhood includes living with the mother, this is the deepest shame of my life, and its abiding regret. I sat in my chair and spoke into the phone of the pain in my soul, and she listened, and talked to me, and finally said: "You're supposed to be happy. It's your hero's birthday."

I laughed with my whole heart at the humor of it, at the truth of it, and now my pain was bearable, my sorrow not a well, but drops of water drying in the winter room.

In March, I decided one day that I must stop talking to her on the telephone because, while I did, I was amused, interested, passionate, joyful; then I said good-bye and I was a cripple who had been sitting in his wheelchair or lying on his bed, holding plastic to his ear. I told her that if I were whole, and could hang up the telephone and walk out of the house, I would not stop calling her; but I knew that living this way, receiving her by telephone, was not a good crippled way to live; and I knew there was a better crippled way to live, but I did not know yet what it was. She understood; she always does, whether or not she agrees.

I did not call her for days, and on the first day of April, I woke crying, and on the second; and on the third, I could not stop, and I phoned my doctor's receptionist and, still crying, I told her to tell him to give me a shot or put me away someplace, because I could not bear it anymore. At noon, he brought me spinach pie and chili dogs, and I said: "That's cholesterol."

"Depression will kill you sooner," he said, and I ate with him and still did not understand that the food and his presence at my table were sacraments. He made an appointment for me with a psychologist, and two days later my youngest son drove me to the office of this paternal and compassionate man, who said: "This is not depression; it's sorrow, and it'll always be with you, because you can't replace your legs."

As my son drove me home, I told him that I wanted a swimming pool, but I did not want to be a man who needed a swimming pool to be happy.

He said: "You're not asking the world for a swimming pool. You're asking it for motion."

At home, I called a paraplegic friend and asked him to teach me to drive my car, and two days later he did. I phoned a swimming pool contractor, a durably merry and kind man, and his cost for building me a forty-by-fifteen-by-three-foot lap pool was so generous that I attribute it to gimpathy. Sacraments abounded. I paid for some, and the money itself was sacramental: my being alive to receive it and give it for good work. On that first day, after calling the paraplegic and the contractor, I called the woman, and I continued to call her, and to receive that grace.

On the last day of my father's life, he was thirsty and he asked me to crush some ice and feed it to him. I was a Marine captain, stationed at Whidbey Island, Washington, and I had flown home to Lake Charles, Louisiana, to be with my father before he died, and when he died, and to bury him. I did not know then that the night flight from Seattle was more than a movement in air from my wife and four young children to my dying father, that every moment of it, even as I slept, was a sacrament I gave my father; and they were sacraments he gave me, his siring and his love drawing me to him through the night; and sacraments between my mother and two sisters and me, and all the relatives and friends I was flying home to; and my wife and children and

me, for their love was with me on the plane and I
loved them and I would return to them after burying my father; and from Time itself, God's mystery we often do not clearly see; there was time
now to be with my father. Sacraments came from
those who flew the plane and worked aboard it
and maintained it and controlled its comings and
goings; and from the major who gave me emergency leave, and the gunnery sergeant who did my
work while I was gone. I did not know any of this. I
thought I was a son flying alone.

My father's cancer had begun in his colon, and
on the Saturday before the early Sunday morning
when he died, it was consuming him, and he was
thin and weak on his bed, and he asked for ice. In
the kitchen, I emptied a tray of ice cubes onto a
dish towel and held its four corners and twisted it,
then held it on the counter and with a rolling pin
pounded the ice till it was crushed. This is how my
father crushed ice, and how my sisters and I, when
we were children, crushed it and put it in a glass
and spooned sugar on it, to eat on a hot summer
day. I put my father's ice into a tall glass and
brought it with an iced-tea spoon to the bedroom
and fed him the ice, one small piece at a time, until
his mouth and throat were no longer dry.

As a boy, I was shy with my father. Perhaps he was
shy with me too. When we were alone in a car,
we were mostly silent. On some nights, when a
championship boxing match was broadcast on the

radio, we listened to it in the living room. He took me to wrestling matches because I wanted to go, and he told me they were fake, and I refused to believe it. He took me to minor-league baseball games. While we listened to boxing matches and watched wrestling and baseball, we talked about what we were hearing and seeing. He took me fishing and dove hunting with his friends, before I was old enough to shoot; but I could fish from the bank of a bayou, and he taught me to shoot my air rifle; taught me so well that, years later, my instructors in the Marine Corps simply polished his work. When I was still too young to use a shotgun, he learned to play golf and stopped fishing and hunting, and on Saturdays and Sundays he brought me to the golf course as his caddy. I did not want to caddy, but I had no choice, and I earned a dollar and a quarter; all my adult life, I have been grateful that I watched him and listened to him with his friends, and talked with him about his game. My shyness with him was a burden I did not like carrying, and I could not put down. Then I was twenty-one and a husband and a Marine, and on the morning my pregnant wife and I left home, to drive to the Officers' Basic School in Quantico, Virginia, my father and I tightly embraced, then looked at each other's damp eyes. I wanted to say *I love you*, but I could not.

I wanted to say it to him before he died. On the afternoon of his last day, he wanted bourbon and water. A lot of ice, he told me, and a lot of water. I made drinks for my sister and me too, and brought his in a tall glass I did not hold for him. I do not remember whether he lifted it to his mouth or rested it on his chest and drank from an angled hospital straw. My sister and I sat in chairs at the foot of the bed, my mother talked with relatives and friends in the living room and brought them in to speak to my father, and I told him stories of my year of sea duty on an aircraft carrier, of my work at Whidbey Island. Once he asked me to light him a cigarette. I went to his bedside table, put one of his cigarettes between my lips, lit his Zippo, then looked beyond the cigarette and flame at my father's eyes: they were watching me. All my life at home before I left for the Marine Corps, I had felt him watching me, a glance during a meal or in the living room or on the lawn, had felt he was try-ing to see my soul, to see if I was strong and hon-orable, to see if I could go out into the world, and live in it without him. His eyes watching me light his cigarette were tender, and they were saying good-bye.

That night, my father's sisters slept in the beds that had been mine and my sister's, and she and I went to the house of a neighbor across the street. We did not sleep. We sat in the kitchen and drank and cried, and I told her that tomorrow I would tell my father I loved him. Before dawn he died, and for years I regretted not saying the words. But I did not understand love then, and the sacraments that make it tactile. I had not lived enough and lost enough to enable me to know the holiness of working with meat and mustard and bread; of moving on wheels or wings or by foot from one place to another; of holding a telephone and speaking into it and listening to a voice; of pounding ice with wood and spooning the shards onto a dry tongue; of lighting a cigarette and placing it between the fingers of a man trying to enjoy tobacco and bourbon and his family as he dies.

Bodily Mysteries

NEARLY FIVE YEARS AGO, A CAR STRUCK me. I lost one leg above the knee and the use of the other, so I am confined to a wheelchair. Every day I long for what I used to do: standing, walking, going on long conditioning walks. A little more than a year after the accident, my marriage ended; my two daughters, eight and four now, live with their mother. I am with them often, but they rarely spend the night with me. So most mornings, I wake up alone. Each day is a struggle against sorrow, with every physical action in the empty house showing me again and again what I have lost. I cannot win this struggle alone.

I am writing this on a Wednesday. The past five days have been bad ones, and I have prayed in desperation, prayed for strength, hope, love, gratitude. This morning I resumed my physical contact with God: I went to Mass and received the Eucharist. For a Catholic, the Eucharist is the body and blood of Jesus Christ in the form of bread and wine. Since I was a boy, this sacrament has sustained my belief in God, who joined us here on earth to eat and drink and be joyful, to love and grieve, to suffer and die. For most of my life, I have tried to receive the Eucharist daily.

But during the past year or more, overwhelmed by my body and my spirit, I have rarely gone to daily Mass. I pray that from now on I will. For now, I feel peace and joy. I am listening to opera; I am writing. This morning, after struggling with two doors to get into the church, I settled in my chair and watched the priest lifting the unleavened bread, and saying, "This is my body"; lifting the chalice of wine, saying, "This is my blood of the new covenant" . . . and peace of mind came to me and, yes, happiness too, for I was no longer a broken body, alone in my chair. I was me, all of me, in wholeness of spirit. The old man assisting the priest handed me the Host, and I placed it in my mouth and was in harmony with the old man, the priest, the walking communicants passing me and my chair to receive the Eucharist; one with all people in pain and joy and passion, one with the physical universe, with Christ, with the timeless dimension of the spirit, which has no past or future but only now; one with God. Me: flawed and foolish me. I drove my car to church and consumed God.

A Country Road
Song

ON A COUNTRY ROAD IN BRADFORD,
Massachusetts, there is a hill without trees in
a meadow. It is two miles from an apartment where
I lived alone, and, after writing in the morning, I
ran on the asphalt road, went through a wooden
gate, ran on grass to the hill, then slowly ran up it.
It is a deceptive hill, and a friend who sometimes
ran with me named it Agony Hill. I ran to a crest
and looked up at another, and ran to that one and
looked up at another; at the top, I stood, sweating
and breathing fast and deeply, and looked across
the field at a long, curving stretch of the Merrimack River, and a line of trees at its bank. I ran up

this hill in all seasons, unless there was snow on the earth.

Sometimes I drove to Lake Kenoza in Haverhill, and ran on a dirt trail in woods. The trail followed the lake and turned up a long hill, and I ran up it and looked down between trees at the water and ran down, and back along the trail, and came out of the woods, and, before going to the water fountain and my car, I ran up a short, steep hill, a very good sledding hill when snow covers it. I named this Marine Green Hill, after a friend running up it behind me yelled: "Up that hill, Marine; up that hill," and suddenly I was eighteen years old again, running up a hill at Quantico, Virginia, and a Marine sergeant was yelling, giving my legs, my lungs, my will the push they needed.

One very cold and windy and sunlit day, I ran on a country road, then on a neighborhood street toward home, and saw ahead of me a woman I knew. She was walking toward me. She was in her sixties then, and I knew that every Sunday she walked at Rye Beach, and often I thought of her walking in snow at the edge of the sea. She worked at Bradford College, where I taught; she worked at the switchboard, and one day in my first spring in New England, I ran into the building, out of cold rain, and said to her: "When is spring coming?" and she said: "This is spring." Now in the cold wind, we approached each other; she wore an overcoat and gloves and a scarf around her head and ears.

Her cheeks were red. She waved, and called into the wind: "Where is everyone? Why are you and I the only ones out here, on this beautiful day?"

It was a beautiful day, and I believe she and I were outdoors not because of pride or discipline, but love. For fifteen years in New England, I ran in all seasons to exercise my body, because exercising my body cleared my brain, and gave me joy. Then for five years, I walked fast but without lengthening my stride, inhaling for three steps, holding my breath for three, exhaling for three; it was peaceful, and I loved it more than running. On a warm spring day, on a road between Bradford and Boxford, I was walking past a line of trees and I heard above me the low sound of something hard, in motion, striking something soft at rest, and a squeal of terror that I felt in my body, and I looked up, to see a hawk flying up from a branch, with a sparrow in its talons, climbing in the blue sky. Sometimes, walking among meadows and trees, I sang. Once in summer, while singing "I Get a Kick Out of You," I passed a farmhouse and a woman opened the front door and called: "Far *out.*"

I was. When I ran, when I walked, there was no time: there was only my body, my breath, the trees and hills and sky, the birds and chipmunks and squirrels, the cold or hot or cool air, the rain on my hat and face, the white and silent motion of snow. The rhythm of running and walking and deep breathing soothed my soul, and the landscapes and weather thrilled it. I always felt grateful, but I did not know it was gratitude, and so I never thanked God, or the leaves, or air, or my legs. Eight years ago, on a starlit night in July, a car hit me, and I was in a hospital for seven weeks, and in September the surgeon cut off my left leg, at the middle of the knee, and I went home with my right leg in a full cast that would not come off till June. The femur and tibia of my right leg had been shattered, the nerves were damaged, the muscles atrophied and tightened with scar tissue, and my knee would not bend. It still does not. I worked with physical therapists for three years, exercising my leg, walking with an artificial leg and crutches, trying to strengthen muscles and bend my knee. Walking with my right leg and an artificial one was harder than anything I have ever done with my body. Finally, I knew it was time to stop going for three hours three times a week to physical therapy; time to expect my leg to be no more than an often-painful limb that I am glad I have, for it keeps me five feet and nine inches long, and it is mine; time to accept life in a wheelchair. In summer, I swim; some days in fall and spring, I push myself around the church parking lot, singing. In all seasons, I play Sinatra on compact discs, and in my chair I sing with him, and shadowbox and dance.

It is time now to sing of my gratitude: for legs and hills and trees and seasons. Spring here comes at its own pace, and without consistence. It comes as rain, snow, sunlight, days of gray sky, and buds are on tree branches, and the grass is green. I ran and walked in sweatpants and sweatshirt till I no longer needed them; then I wore shorts and a T-shirt and a folded bandanna tied around my head to keep sweat from my eyes. Then it was summer and I wore only the shorts and bandanna, the shoes and socks, and loved the feel of sweat coming out of my body, dripping on my skin, and I felt that these long sunlit days would keep coming, one after another after another after another. I ran or walked five miles and went into my house, my socks damp, my shorts wet, and I wrung sweat from the bandanna, and ate tomatoes grown in this earth that months ago was frozen. In fall, the sweat dried more quickly on my skin, and dead leaves gathered on the ground, and the taste and smell of the air were the taste and smell of change. The sun moved toward the tops of distant trees sooner than in summer, poised at their crowns, lighting the sky with red and orange and gold, and the leaves were red and yellow, moving like benevolent flames in the air.

In November, if I ran or walked to the west in late afternoon, the low sun shone straight into my eyes, and in December, late afternoon was dark. For me, it is not the cold air that makes winter long and sometimes sorrowful, but the darkness: the early twilight and dusk, and the nights that seem longer than night should ever be. I wore thermal underwear, a T-shirt, sweatpants and sweatshirt, a light parka that shielded me from the wind, mittens and a ski cap, and if the wind was strong and very cold, I spread vaseline on my face, from my beard to my eyes. And I sweated, running or walking on gray asphalt, up and down hills with brown grass and bare trees and evergreens, and past brown fields. I ran or walked in snow gently floating down, or falling fast as rain, or swirling in the wind: I smelled it and tasted it and sometimes it froze on my beard, and my sweat did too, and they formed tiny icicles. Then there was sunlight for days and I passed meadows of glaring snow, and woods where snow was shaded by pines and bright under trees without leaves. In spring, water ran down hills to the roads, and down them to ditches and lowlands and the river, where melting ice floated to the sea, and I did not wear the parka and mittens and cap, and finally I did not wear the sweatpants and sweatshirt; I ran or walked in shorts and T-shirt, with the bandanna around my head, under a blue sky that in a few days or weeks would host a sun so warm that, save for shorts and socks and shoes, I could run or walk naked on the green earth.

I mourn this, and I sing in gratitude for loving this, and in gratitude for all the roads I ran on and walked on, for the hills I climbed and descended, for trees and grass and sky, and for being spared losing running and walking sooner than I did: ten years sooner, or eight seasons, or three; or one day.

Carrying

IT IS A SATURDAY AFTERNOON IN JUNE, and most of our family is gathered at my house to celebrate the tenth birthday of my daughter Cadence. The sky is blue, the air is dry, and we can sit by the pool without sweating. The water is cool. Pat is with us: she is my first wife and has driven from western Massachusetts for the party. Three of our grown children are here: Suzanne and Andre and Jeb; Nicole is living in California. They are thirty-three, thirty-two, thirty-one, and twenty-nine. Pat must have been tired for years in her twenties, when our children were very young. I only think of this now because being in a wheelchair has made fatigue a part of my life I must outwit. Andre's wife, Fontaine, is here, and Suzanne's boyfriend, Tom, and our friends Tina and Jack. Cadence and Madeleine are the children from my third marriage; Madeleine is five, and their young nanny, Lynda, is here.

Earlier in the week, I asked Cadence what she wanted for dinner at the family party. Child of a divorce, and connected by blood to her father's first marriage, she is today celebrating for the third time in three days: Thursday was her birthday and one of my days with her, and Lynda and Madeleine and I gave her presents, and Suzanne joined us for dinner on her way home from work in Boston. Friday, she went with her mother and Madeleine and a friend from school to lunch in a Japanese restaurant where the chef cooked at the table. She said she wanted pizza on Saturday. But in the pool, my sons are talking to her. The water is three feet deep and they stand and push her on a blue float and their faces are collusive. I sit in my wheelchair near the pool and hear *chicken, sausage, charcoal.*

The women are in lounge chairs in the sun and Tom sits in shade at the picnic table; a beach umbrella is above the table, its shaft in a hole Andre cut in the wood. Beyond the pool, toward the road, green bushes and trees hide the tree house Andre and Jeb and Jack built for Cadence on her ninth birthday. Across the road are wetlands and woods and a long green hill where cows graze. From the float on the water, Cadence says: "Dad? Can we have sausage and chicken on the grill? Instead of pizza?"

The boys volunteer to go to the grocery store. They resist taking my money, but I give it to them and they leave, and Lynda goes inside to make barbecue sauce. Two doves perch on the power line above the driveway. Plastic bottles of sunscreen are scattered about, and we are all anointed. I look at Pat and think of her sunbathing on lawns when we were young, in California and Iowa, New Hampshire and Massachusetts. A woman who was Dorothy Day's friend said that lying in the sun is giving glory to God. Pat and I smoked Pall Malls and Lucky Strikes and ate whatever we wanted to, if we could buy it, and happily went outdoors to be in the sun. It was grand to take heedlessly such pleasures; God knows what damage, if any, we did to our bodies, but perhaps our innocence allowed us to widen our embrace of the earth. Andre has Fontaine, and our unmarried children live with their lovers—Nicole's is a woman—and I do not know that they are all safe, but I feel that they are. Cadence and Madeleine, laughing now in the pool, will have to go with shields into the passion that waits to heat their blood and open them to the virus.

My sons are fathers. Jeb's son is eleven, and Andre's child is in Fontaine's womb. Two weeks ago, Fontaine and Andre showed the sonogram to Cadence and Madeleine and me: the eleven-week-old child Fontaine believes is a girl, and we looked at the arms and legs and eyes. Since then, I have looked differently at Andre. *His wife is pregnant* or *he's a father-to-be* don't apply now. He has grown from the baby I held to a man who married a dark-skinned dancer, and made love with her, hoping she would conceive. He is a father.

In late afternoon, we eat the sausage and chicken at the picnic table. Then Suzanne and Andre and Jeb go into the house and come out and down the ramps to the pool, carrying cartons of ice cream, and presents, and the cake Suzanne has made. Lighted candles are on the cake, and we sing "Happy Birthday" to Cadence, and she blows out the flames. She opens presents from everyone who was not here Thursday; then all of us but Fontaine and Tina go up the ramp to the house. The two women sit in chairs by the pool, facing the sun, which is low over the trees across the road. Jeb and Jack leave, for a concert in Boston. The rest of us go to the sundeck at the side of the house. Beside it on the lawn is the big swing set Jeb and I built for his son and Cadence, when I had legs, before Madeleine was conceived. We worked for three days, digging in the earth, mixing a ton of cement for foundations, hauling beams and cutting and bolting them. On the lawn in front of the deck is the girls' yellow playhouse with green trim. Beyond it, the grass and earth are wet above the leaching field; today in the sun and still air, its stench is faint. Next week, I must call someone to heal this. The deck is without shadows, and the sun is orange.

Andre wants to play catch. The girls' ball is a little smaller than a soccer ball; it is red and yellow, and soft enough to pinch. Madeleine stays with me, and the others go down the steps to the lawn, and arrange themselves on the far side of the swings, and throw: Andre to me, and I toss it to Madeleine, who is standing at the top of the steps; she throws it down to Andre, he throws, and the ball moves in the sunlit air above the grass, to Tom to Cadence to Suzanne to Pat to Andre. Then he looks up at me and says: "Do you want to come down? I can carry you."

I do not know. I have not been on the lawn since Cadence was four and Madeleine was in her mother's womb; I want to be down there with my family. I do not like being carried; I either feel more frangible now or I know how frangible we all are. My injury has led me to people with injuries I never considered when I was whole; I am afraid of falling, of being paralyzed. And being carried frightens me in ways I cannot name; perhaps the absolute surrender to another human being dramatizes for me the dangers I can no longer ward off or evade. I know Andre will not fall or drop me; still I feel all of this. Cadence says: "Yeah, Dad, *please?*"

I say yes. Andre and Pat come up to the deck. He

crouches in front of me, between my leg and stump, and encircles them with his arms; I put mine over his shoulders, and clasp my hands at his chest. I do not know what I weigh; probably I am forty pounds heavier than he is. He stands, lifting me from the chair; my leg and stump, my belly and chest and arms feel his hard muscles. Pat is holding the chair, and walking backward down the steps. Then Andre slowly descends. On the lawn, Pat holds the chair while Andre lowers me into it. He pushes me over the grass and earth, past the swings, and turns me to face the sun setting over the trees across the road.

We throw the ball; sometimes it rolls onto the wet grass and black mud, and we laugh and call out in mock disgust, and someone wipes it clean on dry grass. My children are not content simply to throw the ball and catch it; they like games with results. Soon we are counting each catch; when someone misses, we start over: one, two *three* . . . The sun is near the top of the trees; in front of the house, at the side of the pool, Fontaine and Tina sit and talk; we cannot hear their voices. The pool is in shadow now, from the trees that hold Cadence's tree house. The red-and-yellow ball arcs from our hands, shadows darken the wetlands across the road, and mosquitoes come. We slap and scratch our skin, throw the ball, and count our catches; the air is cooling, and Fontaine and Tina stand and gather their sunscreen and towels. The sun is behind the trees, the sky at their crowns rose and orange; above us, evening's violet spreads, and beneath it is the palest of blue, and we see stars. We want to be in the house now, and Andre pushes me to the steps and squats in front of me. I hold him, and he climbs.

Girls

ALTAR GIRL, AT SUNDAY MASS I WATCH you: your young face, your long brown hair, your white dress. Your skin is light brown; maybe people in your family crossed the Mediterranean, then the Atlantic. Or maybe the Caribbean, but I think the Mediterranean, and I think you are ten years old. Or nine or eight. Your posture is good, your hands graceful. And here you are, sitting on a pew at the side of the altar; kneeling; standing.

You remind me of Mary. In *America* magazine, John F. Kavanaugh wrote that Mary was the first priest. In her body, God became human life. She carried this life, and in labor pushed Him out of her. If you and I did not believe that, we would not be here, and I would not be seeing the only altar girl I have ever seen.

We believe in a woman who, as a girl, said yes to an angel, and had to say yes to a census, and travel there and find a shelter where she could have a baby an angel told her was the Son of God. How much of this could she have believed in the pain of labor, and in her fear? For she must have been afraid of being away from home, of pain, of death, hers or her child's, or both. How much could she believe when she gave birth to her son, and her pain ended, and she held her son and loved Him as she had never loved before? Knowing she would lose Him because he was God; knowing this not every minute but from time to time in his boyhood, when she was able to know with her whole heart and mind and soul that this boy she loved was God.

And how do you love God, who came from your womb and is your son and needs your love and food and teaching and needs to be told it is time to sleep? She did all of this for Him, yet He is God and before she was, He is, and often her heart must have been dazed. He needed her love and she existed because of His.

We do not know whether He ever told her she would lose Him on a cross. You and I, altar girl, see the cross as a sign of love. For her, it was wood and a dying son and grief. And her son was her God. She embodied for all of us the miracle and the mystery and the conflict, the flow and ebb of faith.

You remind me of Mary, altar girl, because you

have a womb, and the moon knows you are here, watching God become bread or bread become God, and your heart too must at times be dazed. You are a girl with a girl's life to live, and you know yourself better than anyone else does, what you think and feel and imagine and want, and all of those are with you in all their significance as you watch the priest consecrate the bread and the wine and now, like Mary, you are looking at Christ. Looking at Christ is believing that Mary gave birth to Him and lived with Him, sometimes knowing, sometimes not knowing, but always Mary, with dark hair and dark skin, thinking and feeling and imagining, sleeping, dreaming, with God in her house, laughing too, under the sun, under the moon.

Liv Ullmann
in Spring

IN MY SIXTH SPRING AFTER BECOMING
crippled, I learned this: as each season ends, I
suffer again the loss of what I used to look forward
to in the season that is coming. It took a long time
to learn, because these feelings are not caused by
images: I do not, as summer ends, imagine hunting
in woods in the fall, then feel sad. Spring may come
with snow, and I may be shut in for days because
there is ice on the driveway up my hill, and I may
be aware only of that. But my body knows that in
summer it will not be walking with children on the
beach, or running into the surf. For days or weeks,
I feel close to crying; and I am afraid, as though

something real and bad is likely to happen very soon; and I am tense, my spirit stretched so tautly that not being able to reach the measuring cup on a shelf could snap it, and having a tire go flat while driving on the road would be a calamity. It is a condition, and I know it will come, and there is nothing to do but wait for it to pass.

In my seventh spring, I went to the Literary Lights dinner, a fund-raiser for the Boston Public Library: people paid a hundred and fifty dollars, and several writers who did not have to pay were invited, and I was one of those, and I could bring a guest. A woman who is the publicity director for my publisher told me on the phone that I was invited, and I said that probably I would not go, because beneath it all I am a shy boy, and eating with adult strangers was frightening to imagine. I also did not want to go because the men would be wearing tuxedos. My feelings about tuxedos are so strong that they are not rational; they make me think of both snobbery and servility; and of freedom too, my own, because usually the wearing of one is ordained. I said to the woman that if I did go to the dinner, I would not wear a tuxedo. She said I could wear whatever I wanted to, which left depending on the kindness of strangers at a dinner table as my only reason to stay away. Styron would be the after-dinner speaker, and my friend Tim O'Brien would be there, and I wanted to hear Styron, and I imagined having drinks before dinner with Tim, look-

ing up at his intensity, his passion, and laughing
with him. My daughter Suzanne told me it was a
good cause. For a few days, I sat with these reasons
to go, and reached my last reason not to go: I
needed someone to drive.

In my third spring after being hit by a car, I
learned to drive with hand controls, and during
the next year and a half, I drove a few times to
Boston at night. It is forty miles south. Then one
night in autumn, when I was supposed to meet
someone in Boston, I was afraid to drive on the
highway and I stayed home. I have not driven to
Boston, alone at night, since then. I am now trying
to gather courage to do it again, for what I am missing in Boston may be worth my fear while driving
there and back, on the highway where I got hit,
on the highway with the feckless drivers of Massachusetts, who frightened and enraged me when I
drove unhurt and whole among them. My fear of
injury and more hospital time or death is aided
and abetted by other people: you cannot drive on
Massachusetts highways without seeing dangerous
drivers; since my accident, I have peacefully been
in cars in Washington and Oregon, Maine and
Connecticut, and Louisiana. So my terror is not
only inside of me; it is also out there: drivers who
seem either to want to die or to believe they cannot, and who seem not to care whether they kill
or harm anyone. I could drive happily at night to
Boston if that wide highway were there only for me,

driving alone with my flares under the car seat, a first-aid kit in my glove compartment, a cellular phone because I cannot walk away from my car if something happens, the something I always anticipate, and a battery with a reserve; I have only to open the hood and turn a switch and the battery will function again, so the car will, the phone will, and the machine that lifts my chair to a box on the car roof and lowers it again will; if the battery is dead while my chair is already up in the box, I will have to crawl on the ground to the front of the car, and to reach the battery, I will have to—I do not know yet.

So, if I decided to go to the dinner, I wanted someone to drive. I told all of this to my friend Jack, who rents my downstairs room and bath, and he said it sounded like fun and he would like to go and he did not have a problem with tuxedos. This was in winter. The dinner would be on the twenty-eighth of March, and I agreed to go. In February, the invitation and the list of guest writers came in the mail, and on the list was Liv Ullmann. Now I wanted to go: I would talk to Tim and listen to Styron and meet Liv Ullmann, and thank her for all the pleasure she has given me in Ingmar Bergman's movies.

Spring came with snowstorms, deep beautiful snow I looked at through my windows and glass doors. For eight days, I was shut in because of ice on the driveway; I knew I could drive down the hill, but my car would not get up it again, to the curb at its top, where I lower my wheelchair and climb onto it and push up six ramps to my kitchen door. It was strange to be inside for so long without being sick. Then it rained and I got out of the house to drive to the machine at the bank, where I can get money while sitting in the car; and to the Book Rack in Newburyport, where the women bring books to the car because I cannot wheel into the store. So I did not get out, as I would if I could walk, but I drove with my window down and the heater on, cold air caressing my face, and I looked at different landscapes and houses and people. Then it snowed again and the water from thaw and rain froze and I stayed inside for five days.

The dinner was on a Sunday, and rain fell, and in the gray afternoon I lay on my bed in the agony of spring. In midafternoon, fog came, and I wanted to cancel, to phone them and use the fog spreading above the ground as an excuse to stay home with fog in my soul, and watch a movie on video, and sleep. We were supposed to leave at five, to be there at six-thirty for an hour of drinks before the dinner. I fell asleep and woke in panic at five, the house dark, and I wheeled to the downstairs door and called to Jack; he was asleep too. I showered upstairs and he showered downstairs and I put on a shirt and sweatpants, a sock and a moccasin, a beret and a Boston Red Sox jacket; he put on a rented tuxedo and gleaming shoes and a raincoat, and in twenty-five minutes we were in my car, Jack at the wheel. I had my leather shoulder bag; it is a possibles bag, for people who shoot muzzle-loaders, and in its front pocket I had a tranquilizer. This is not something I keep in my bag, but I was afraid at the dinner I might yell at someone, or suddenly weep. Light rain fell, and fog was thick on the highway, and I smoked and watched for the car that would hit us. I said: "This is awful."

"What?" He looked happy, as he should have: a healthy bachelor going to eat a free dinner in the company of women. Possibilities were beyond the fog.

"I feel like I'm about to cry. And I feel like I'm riding to a place where some guys are going to beat the shit out of me."

"Did you pray?"

"I'm praying now."

I imagined a large room filled with standing people holding drinks, and suddenly knew what I should have known when I saw Liv Ullmann's name on the list: I would not be able to meet her. I can no longer move subtly between people, and I did not know how significant sidling is, and skirting is, and weaving is, until in my wheelchair I first encountered a crowded room, and tried to enjoy the party. One person standing in front of me keeps me from seeing other people; I cannot easily excuse myself and wander about, talking with different people. Everyone has to move out of my way, and often I have to ask them to, and they do not always step aside. Some men glance down at me, then look back at the person they are talking to, and I have to say, "Excuse me," and sometimes nudge their bodies with my moving chair. They do not seem callous so much as uncomfortable. Only educated men have treated me this way. Working-class men have treated me simply as an injured human being, have greeted me, stepped aside, and offered help. Women in general have been kind. I do not understand what this means about some men in suits. In the room where we would have drinks before dinner, people would be standing close to one another, there would be no swaths three feet wide leading to Liv Ullmann; and sitting in the car, waiting for death or injury to come speeding through rain and fog, I saw myself in that room, looking up at the backs of men and women, my mouth closed while my heart bellowed: Is Liv Ullmann in there? Is she among you? Will you please make way for me?

The dinner was at the Park Plaza hotel and we would have been there at six-thirty, but outside of Boston there was traffic you could walk past, and I watched the digital clock on the dashboard, and felt I had failed other people; and everything I felt was more than I could bear. There was nothing to do but look at the stopped or very slow cars, and the rain and fog, so there was nothing to do but bear it. If I had not felt all of this so many times before, I might have believed it was the beginning of a nervous breakdown. It is so much better to know that something will end, and I knew that if I could hold on for the night, perhaps with a tranquilizer, tomorrow morning would be different. Maybe it would only be different, not better, but today would be in the past, and I would be at home.

We got to the Park Plaza at seven-fifteen and Jack parked vertically, backing the car to a high curb. He held my chair while I pulled myself onto it; then he backed me to the curb, stepped up on it, and tilted me back at a forty-five-degree angle. He started to pull me up to the sidewalk and, while I was off the ground, his feet slipped, and he gained his balance and lowered me to the street. He said it was his rented shoes, on the wet cement. A young black boy stood on the sidewalk, watching us. He stepped forward and said: "Can I help you?"

Jack asked him to get in front of me and lift as he pulled; they did, and I was on the sidewalk. In the hotel, we went up an elevator, then over a carpeted floor to the hall leading to the room where the people were gathered for drinks. The writers got flowers: a woman in charge of the evening pinned a white rose on my shirt, and I apologized for being late, and she said the fog had made a lot of people late, and there was plenty of time before dinner. The room with the bar was to the left of the hall, and there were two doors. We went to the first one: people were crowded near the door and beyond, so we went to the second. I could get through it without asking anyone to move, and we went through and skirted the crowd and stopped near the bar at one end of the room. I sat with my leg elevated at ninety degrees on the wheelchair's leg rest; when I lower my leg, it hurts, and the circulation is bad, and my foot becomes red, then purple. I looked at the standing people, at their backs and profiles, and Jack brought me a vodka and tonic from the bar. On a table in front of me was a display of books by the writers who were guests. I could not see Tim in the crowd, or space in it, or Liv Ullmann. Behind me were the closed doors of the dining room and, much later, when they opened the doors and we went in and I was at a table, I went to the bathroom, and Tim was there. He used the urinal on the wall, and I used the one I carry hooked by its handle to the leg rest of my chair. He said: "Why aren't you wearing a tuxedo? I'm wearing a fucking tuxedo."

"I'm a civilian now," I said. "People can't tell me what to wear anymore."

We laughed and smoked and talked, then went back to the dining room. His table was near Liv Ullmann's and Tim could see her face. I could not see her from my table, but by then I had met her.

Soon after I got into the bar and sat in the open space, a woman from a newspaper came to me and told me her name and we talked. I said I wanted to meet Liv Ullmann.

"Would you like me to find her?"

"I'd love you to find her."

She went out the door I had come through from the hall, and soon she was back, looking happy.

"She's right there," she said. "In the hall, with her husband and someone else."

"Only two people? In the hall?"

I pushed my wheels and Jack pushed and we went through the door and turned right, and there she was, at the hall's entrance, where the woman had greeted me with a rose. She was talking to a woman, and I wheeled to them and stopped, looked up at the left side of her face, and waited. Her husband stood to my left. I sat looking up at her art: the ennui and grief, the delight and passion and agony of Bergman's long and beautiful struggle. Then she turned and looked down at me and smiled. In her blue eyes I saw my pain. I reached with my right hand and she took it and held it. I said: "I want to thank you for all the pleasure you've given me."

She smiled and thanked me, and I released her hand and slowly backed away. I said: "I know what it's like to be talked to in public. So I only wanted to tell you that."

Her eyes held me, and I could not look away from her compassion. She stepped toward me; I stopped the chair, and said: "I feel like it's all a dream. But it's someone else's dream. And what will happen when he wakes up and feels guilty?"

She looked as she might if I had told her a good secret about her life, and she gazed deeply into me and said: "You *know* that?"

"You said it, near the end of *Shame*."

Her lips opened, her cheeks moved, her eyes looked at me, and at years of her life. Then she said: "It's been part of my thinking for years. I had forgotten it was in a film."

"Yes. I forget my stories."

She glanced at the rose pinned to my shirt, then looked at my eyes, and I was looking back at years of my own life. She leaned toward me and said "Do you have a book? Here?"

"Yes."

"Let's sign our books to each other."

"The ones on display? Will they let us?"

"They'll have to."

I turned and started to wheel to the hall and she stepped behind me and put a hand on my shoulder. I stopped and looked up and to my right at her face.

"I want to introduce you to my husband."

She did; he looked kind and cheerful, and I reached back to shake his hand, my arm under hers; then I looked at her face. She was bent low, and my breast filled, and quickly in a low voice I told her everything: being hit by a car, the long hospital time, the loss each morning waking from dreams of myself with legs, the end of the seasons' loss of walking in the season to come, that very day's fear and sorrow, and all of it went out of me, into her hand on my shoulder, and her eyes looking at mine. She said: "You cannot compensate."

"No," I said. "I cannot compensate."

Then my breast filled with peace. We went down the hall and through the second floor, into the room with the bar, and to the table where our books were. They were next to each other. She knew that with her body she could dispel my isolation: in the hall, she had leaned close to me; now she crouched to write in her book. I could look straight at her face. Later, during dinner, the woman who had pinned on the rose would bring Liv's book to me, and mine to her.

We shook hands. The peace in my heart remained, brimmed, was joy; and enjoyable people were at the dinner table, and I felt love for everyone, even for myself. This stayed with me for fourteen days and nights, and every day and night I thought of her, and was grateful. I thought of sending her flowers, of inviting her and her husband to dinner. After two weeks, my fear and sadness returned one morning, were there when I opened my eyes. But in three days, they were gone; the sun shone day after day, and at night the air was cool; grass appeared, and leaves, and I wheeled to my desk, to a new notebook, whose cover is colored like peacock feathers, and wrote: Liv Ullmann in Spring.

Love in the Morning

A	T THE WEEKDAY MASS IN MY PARISH
	church, I see the same people, as in a neigh-
borhood bar. Everyone does not come every day,
but I rarely see someone who is not a regular. We
greet one another going in, say good-bye leaving.
One morning when I parked at the church, an old
woman and two old men were standing near the
door I can go through in my wheelchair. I opened
my car door and pressed the switch to open the
box on the roof of my car and lower on two chains
my folded wheelchair. The woman and men were
talking about their bodies, about tests and medica-
tions. My chair descended and the woman looked

at me and smiled and said to the men: "And here comes the one with no troubles at all."

I have been at funeral Masses for people I did not know. When there will be many people at a funeral, that Mass is usually in midmorning, after the daily Mass. Years ago, I walked one morning from my apartment to the early Mass and saw a hearse outside. I went into the sacristy, where the priest was putting on his vestments, and asked him if I should go home. "Oh, no," he said. "It's a very small funeral. Just sit in the back."

"Should I receive Communion?"

"Of course. It's a community. Wait till her family receives, then come."

I knelt in the back. So did the other regulars, when they came in. That was at Sacred Hearts' Church in Bradford, Massachusetts. Now I go to weekday Masses at St. John the Baptist Church in Haverhill, because it is close to my house, Mass is at nine, rather than before eight, and it is the easiest church in town for me to push my wheelchair into. It is a brick church with steps at its front; but at both its sides, close to its rear, there are doors without steps or a curb, and the asphalted ground is level. So I roll in, between the altar and the first pew, and park in the middle aisle.

I have taken part in several funeral Masses here. I push backward in a side aisle till I am at the rear of the church with the other regulars. I would feel like an intruder, if the priest at Sacred Hearts' had not instructed me. Now I see a few relatives and friends in the first six or seven pews, flanking the body in the casket; then the empty pews separating them from the rest of us; the priest at the altar; the brown wooden walls and ceiling, and the stained-glass windows enclosing all of us; and I think it is good for us strangers to be here as witnesses to death and life, to prayer and grief. During the Mass in the church, we are not strangers. We simply do not know one another. Entering the building has rendered us peaceable; the Mass keeps us respectful; we speak only when we pray, and when the priest asks us to offer one another a sign of peace, and we take the hands of those near us and say: "Peace be with you."

The Mass unites us with the body in the casket, and with its soul traversing whatever it is that souls traverse, perhaps visiting now the people in the pews near the body; perhaps melding with infinity, receiving the brilliant love of God. The Mass and the walls and floor and ceiling of the church unite us with the people who knew this person, with their sorrow, like the sorrow most of us have felt and all of us will feel unless we die before anyone we love dies. It unites us with the mortality of our bodies, with the immortality of our souls. The Mass ends and everyone but me stands as the family and friends follow the body in the casket out of the church. Then we leave, and tell each other good-bye. We do not say good-bye. We wave, we nod;

sometimes we say, "Have a good day." Earthly time is upon us again; we enter it, and go to our cars. Sometimes, in spring and fall, I do not go to my car. I push myself around the church, on the asphalt parking lot, downhill on one side of the church, then uphill on the other; I breathe deeply and look at trees and the sky and passing cars, and I sing.

The thirtieth anniversary of John F. Kennedy's murder was a Monday, a day in Massachusetts with a blue sky, and in the morning I filled a quart plastic bottle with water, put on a Boston Red Sox jacket and cap, and a pair of gloves, and went outside and down the six ramps to my car, and drove to the church. On Sunday afternoon, while I was driving my young daughters to their mother's house in a nearby town, the first line of a story had come to me. I was talking with my daughters and watching cars and the road, and suddenly the sentence was inside me; it had come from whatever place they come from. It is not a place I can enter at will; I simply receive its gifts. I had been gestating this story for a very long time, not thinking about it, but allowing it to possess me, and waiting to see these characters living in me: their faces, their bodies. I do not start writing a story until I see the people and the beginning of the story. In the car with my girls, I knew I must start writing the story on Monday, and before writing, I wanted to receive Communion and exercise. So Monday, I drove to the church, grateful to be out of bed and on the way to Mass on a lovely morning, my flesh happily anticipating exercise in the air, under the sun. In that space between my heart and diaphragm was the fear I always feel before writing, when my soul is poised to leap alone.

There is only one priest at the church, and he is the pastor and lives in the small brick rectory beside the church. The rectory faces the street and is close to the sidewalk, and it is separated from the church by a driveway leading to the parking lot, and on some mornings in the basement of the rectory, people in Alcoholics Anonymous gather to help one another. I like this priest, but liking him is not important. A priest can be shallow, boring, shy, arrogant, bigoted, or mean; during Mass, it is not important. I believe most Catholics go to Mass for the same reason I do: to take part in ritual, and to eat the body of Christ. If the priest is an intelligent, humorous, and impassioned speaker, then the Mass includes the thrill of being entertained, even spiritually fed. I know that a homily can affect the soul. But a mute priest could perform a beautiful Mass, and anyone could read aloud the prayers and the Gospel and the words of the Consecration of the bread and wine. The homilies of the priest at St. John the Baptist are good; he always says something I can use that day.

I do not remember his homily on that November Monday morning. At Mass, my mind wanders about like a released small child. It does this wherever I am; it is not mine to hold, and I can either concentrate and so contain it or wait for it to return. Probably at Mass that morning, I was concentrating on not writing the story in my mind, for doing that disturbs the gestation, and the life that may come on the page comes too soon. Once, while working on a novella, I came home from teaching and, before writing, I took my golden retriever outside to relieve himself. It was late afternoon and we walked in a grove of trees on the campus. The dog rolled on the ground and chewed on fallen branches, and the work I meant to do at my desk began coming to me: the people and the words I would use and the rhythms of punctuation. I let it come and it filled me and I was not under a blue sky in the shade of a grove with my happy dog; I was a young woman who lived in a notebook on my desk, and the words I saw and hefted in my mind gave her a body and motion and dread and hope, and I was those too. Then I went inside with the dog and made a cup of tea and went to my desk; but my soul, filled in the grove, was empty. I sat at my desk but did not write. I had already written, without a pen in my hand, standing under trees and gazing at my golden dog. It is part of my vocation not to worry about what I am working on, and never to think about it when I am not at my desk, and doing this demands as much discipline and focus as sitting at my desk and writing. I also keep a notebook and pen with me, everyplace where I am clothed, for those images or people or scenes that may fall on me like drops of rain.

I hope I prayed for my murdered president at Mass; I do not remember. Dead for thirty years, he would not need prayers to help him on that Monday in 1993. But since reading Dorothy Day's belief that prayers for the dead can help them while they were alive on earth, I have believed it. I prayed to Kennedy later in the day, after Mass and exercise and a shower and breakfast, when I wheeled to my desk. I had never prayed to him before. Moments before I wrote the sentence that had come to me in the car with my girls, I prayed: Jack, you were an active man, and probably people don't ask you to do much anymore, so will you help me with this story?

When Mass ended, I put on my jacket and gloves, and hung my leather bag on my right shoulder, the straps angling down my chest and back to the bag on my left thigh, which is now a stump. I left the church and put on the baseball cap and looked up at the blue sky. I went to the passenger side of the car, reached for the bottle of water on the seat, and drank. People got into their cars and drove out of the parking lot. I waited for them to leave; I do not like moving among cars in motion; my body's instincts are to step or jump out of their way, but the chair has no instincts at all. This is something I think about when I am sitting next to the stove, stirring a pot of beans.

When the people in cars were gone, I pushed

uphill to a tree at the edge of the lot. Behind it, the hill had brown grass and rose to a brick nursing home. Three young women sat in chairs outside, smoking in the sunlight. I turned right, and pushed behind the church, singing "Glad to Be Unhappy." I sing while exercising so that I will breathe deeply into my stomach; I also do it because pushing a wheelchair around a parking lot is not exciting, as running and walking were; but singing, combined with the work of muscles and blood, makes it joyful. I know that, to some people, I may seem mad, wheeling up and down and around a parking lot and singing torch songs. But there were no people, and the priest was in the rectory, and I did not care if he heard me; he is a priest, and must be merciful about things more serious than someone singing off-key. It amused me to imagine watching this from the height of a hunting hawk: the nursing home, and downhill from it the church, and the singing man on wheels speeding down and turning right and passing the front of the church, then pushing uphill to the tree. Safety was not the only reason I chose the church parking lot for laps; I did not want anyone to hear me.

The people who heard me arrived in cars a quarter of an hour after I started my laps. They parked near the rectory and gathered at its rear, by the open door of the garage. In the garage are steps to the basement, and at ten o'clock these people would go down there for a meeting. But now they stood talking, men and women, most of them drinking coffee from Styrofoam cups, and smoking. I sang softly as I pushed past them, up the hill, and did not look at their faces. If I looked at their faces, I would not sing. At the tree, I looked up the hill at the three women sitting outside the nursing home, then turned right and sang loudly again and wheeled past the back of the church. All of us were receiving sensual and soothing pleasures: the workers at the nursing home, smoking; the alcoholics, drinking coffee and smoking; me, pushing and singing, after eating the body of Christ. At the end of the parking lot, I turned downhill and steered as the chair rolled fast; to my left were houses, and across the street was the high school football stadium, but not the school, which is in another part of town.

When I came around the church and went up between it and the rectory, I stopped singing and looked at the alcoholics. I felt an affinity for them and believed that, because of their own pain and their desire to mend, they did not see me as an aberrant singer on wheels, but as a man also trying to mend. That was in their faces. They all watched me going by; some of the men greeted me; women smiled and looked. I said: "How y'all doing?" and went up the hill, sweating. I stopped at my car and unlocked the passenger door and drank water. A small gray bus with the engine in front, like a school bus for only a few children, came up the driveway between the rectory and the church. It turned left and stopped and teenaged girls and boys got out, some lit cigarettes, and they all walked down to the gathering of alcoholics. I pushed away from my car and went up to the tree and turned.

Going down the hill toward the street, I saw a man on the sidewalk, to my left; he was walking at a quick pace toward the church. His overcoat was unbuttoned and he wore a coat and white shirt and tie; he had lost hair above his brow, and something about his face made me feel that he did not work in an office. I turned to roll in front of the church; he was walking parallel to me, thirty feet away, and he looked at me. I stopped singing. He was glaring, and I felt a soft rush of fear under my heart, and a readying of myself. He raised his right arm and his middle finger and yelled: "Fuck *God*."

He was looking at the church, walking fast, his finger up. My fear changed; for a moment, I expected a response: the sky suddenly dark gray, thunder, lightning. He yelled it again. We were both opposite the church door, and there was no fear in me now; I wondered if any of the alcoholics or the priest in the rectory were frightened or offended. He yelled again, his finger up; his anger was pure and fascinating. By now I knew he was unsound. We passed the church, and I turned and pushed upward, looking at him over my left shoulder. He kept his finger up as he passed the rectory, still yelling. I moved past the alcoholics watching him; some smiled at me, and I smiled. As I pushed to the top of the parking lot, I looked up at the nursing home. The workers had gone inside. I sang, and laughed as I rolled past the rear of the church, seeing all of us: the roofs of the church and rectory, and the alcoholics talking and smoking, and me singing and sweating in the wheelchair, and the man in the suit and tie, with his finger up as far as he could reach. On that morning under a blue November sky, it was beautiful to see and hear such belief: Fuck *God.*

I wrote the story in four days; it is very short, and I knew before starting it that it was coming like grace to me, and I could receive it or bungle it, but I could not hold it at bay; and if I were not able to receive it with an open heart and, with concentration, write it on paper, it would come anyway, and pass through me and through my room to dissipate in the air, and it might not come back. That is why I prayed to Kennedy. It was strange, in those four days, to become one with the woman in the story, and the evil she chose, and the ecstasy it gave her and me. I called the story "The Last Moon," and in December I wrote it again, and in January I wrote it again. I did not look at it for days between drafts, and worked at not thinking about it, because it was hot and I was hot, and we both needed to cool, so I could see it clearly enough to take words away from it. But in January, it was done, which truly means I had done all I could ever do with it, and it became something that lived apart from me. I started another story, and in a few weeks "The Last Moon" was a memory, much like meeting someone while you are traveling, and you eat and drink and talk with this person, even feel love, and then you go home with the memory and it does not matter to you whether you ever see the person again.

That winter, snow fell and fell and froze and stayed on the ground. The church parking lot was plowed often, but a coating of snow remained, and all winter I did not push my chair around the church. I live on a steep hill, and each time the snow stopped falling, a friend plowed it; then I paid young men to come in a pickup truck and shovel sand onto the driveway. A friend shoveled my ramps and spread rock salt on them and chipped away the ice on top of the railings I used to pull myself upward to the house. Most days that winter I did not go to Mass; I could have gone, on many days, but waking in the morning and thinking of cold air and of rolling on the packed thin layer of snow and ice blunted the frail edge of my desire to leave my warm bed, and I lay in it.

One of the regulars at daily Mass is a pretty blond woman in her thirties. On a cold and gray spring

morning, I drove to the church, and a seventy-
eight-year-old man walked from his car to talk
to me while I lowered my chair. I knew his age
because once I had asked him how old Jack Kennedy would be if he were still alive, and he said:
"Same as me; seventy-eight." On that morning in
spring, after the winter of snow, I got into my chair,
and the blonde drove into the parking lot and
stopped. We looked at her. She walked past us to
the church and smiled and said good morning,
and we did, and she went through the door I use.
The man shook his head, grinning. He said: "If I
were ten minutes younger . . ."

Two days later, he was standing outside when I
drove to the church. The sky was still gray, the air
cold. As I lowered my chair and got the armrest
and seat cushion and leg rest from the backseat, I
watched him. He was looking at the sky, at the
green hill in front of the nursing home, at trees
near the parking lot. I got into my chair and he
looked at me and said: "I'm looking for a robin."

I told him I had seen one that week, on my lawn.

Today is a Friday in early September. It is not
autumn yet, but the air is cool and rain falls, and in
the rain I see winter coming, snow and ice on my
ramps and driveway, on roads and parking lots and
sidewalks, snowbanks pushed by plows to curbs,
blocking the curb cuts I use in my chair; and the
long dark nights. While this September rain falls, I

want to be held, loved; but this morning I woke too late to go to Mass. I have learned rarely to worry about my work, and not to write it in my mind without a pen in my hand and paper in front of me. But I have not learned to live this way, so I sit in September, listening to rain, glancing up from the page at it, feeling the cool air coming through my windows and open glass door, and I feel the sorrow of a season that has not come. This morning, the sky was blue, and if I had gotten out of bed and gone to Mass, I would not feel this sorrow now; it would be there, but as a shadow, among other shadows of pain; the trees that cast these shadows are mortality and failures in love, in faith, in hope; and if I had this morning received the Eucharist, all of these would be small shapes and shadows surrounded by light.

I go to Mass because the Eucharist is there. Before the priest raises the disk of unleavened bread and the chalice of wine and consecrates them and they become Christ, the Eucharist is there in the tabernacle. When it is time for us to receive Communion, the priest will go to the tabernacle and take from it the consecrated Hosts to give to us. But the Eucharist is not only there in the tabernacle. I can feel it as I roll into the church. It fills the church. If the church had no walls, the Eucharist would fill the parking lot, the rectory, the nursing home, the football stadium. And the church has no walls, and the Eucharist fills the women smoking outside the nursing home; and the alcoholics waiting to gather, but already they are gathered, as they are gathered when they are apart; fills the man cursing God from the isolation of his mind; fills the old man watching a woman, and looking for robins. When I am enclosed by the walls and roof and floor, and the prayers and duration of Mass, I see this, and feel it; and when the priest places the Host in the palm of my hand, I put it in my mouth and taste and chew and swallow the intimacy of God.

Song of Pity

IN NOVEMBER AFTER THE GULF WAR, IN
my sixth year as a cripple, I read a newspaper
story about a thirty-four-year-old man: in the summer after the war, while playing rugby, he received
an injury that changed his body, and so his life, forever: he is a quadriplegic. The newspaper story
focused on the good effect he had on his friends
and other people in the city where he lived: they
raised money for him; his friends visited him in the
hospital, and said they drew strength from his
courage. The injured man said he had regained
the use of his hands, and that he would walk; he
said he would play golf. He was still in the hospital.

I was hit by a car on the highway, and I am not paralyzed; and on the night of my injury, I was forty-nine years old and my sixth child was in her mother's womb. Friends visited me, phoned, wrote letters. Eight writers raised money for me with readings at the Charles Hotel in Cambridge; I did not know five of them till we met on the afternoons of their readings. People sent me checks. The quadriplegic was playing a game on grass in summer, and his injury was far worse than mine; as he lay on the ground, after being hurt, he said: "I'm still single."

So why, as I ate cereal and read this story, did I feel rage instead of gratitude? I wanted to yell at someone, above all to put someone in a wheelchair for one long pushing, pulling, turning, reaching, muscle-aching, mind-absorbing day. But who? The reporter and his editor? That newspaper favorably reviews restaurants the quadriplegic cannot go into; in its reviews, the paper does tell you whether or not the restaurant is accessible to people in wheelchairs. This does not mean the reviewers and editors and restaurant owners think of us as people in a democracy. The newspaper would not review a restaurant that was accessible only to Caucasians, or only to men.

The quadriplegic's arms and hands cannot push a wheelchair; his confinement and his mobility will be a chair with a motor. They weigh two hundred and fifty pounds. Who will carry him up even one step to a restaurant? And why would he want to be carried? When you are carried, your helplessness, and the very meatness of you, slap your soul. And it is a frightening surrender to other arms and legs. Chairs with motors cost around eight thousand dollars, and if you plan to leave your home, you need a van with a lift, and someone to drive it; though once I met a quadriplegic who somehow drove. The quadriplegic will not walk. A few years after my crippling, I bought a video of *The Men*, and watched Marlon Brando playing a paraplegic. At his wedding, he stood from his chair, holding on to the pew beside him. Alone on my couch, watching him stand, sweating, on paralyzed legs, I laughed aloud at this dangerous mockery of those of us who cannot; whose spirits are willing, whose flesh will not.

The quadriplegic will be forever dependent on someone. He cannot sit on a toilet, he cannot wipe himself, or shave, shower, make his bed, dress. He will use a catheter. He cannot cook. He will not feel the heat of a woman, except with his face.

When I was a graduate student at the University of Iowa Writers' Workshop, I had a friend in a wheel-chair. I met him in late afternoon on a cold winter day; there was snow on the ground and sidewalks, and he was pushing his chair up a long, steep hill. I was walking perpendicular to him at the bottom of the hill when I heard his voice. I stopped and saw a black man looking over his shoulder at me, calling: "Can you give me a push?"

He could not push farther up the hill. I felt the embarrassment of being whole while he was not, and went up to him and pushed. In this way, we introduced ourselves; I spoke to the back of his head, and he spoke into the cold air in front of him. The hill led to a street that was flat, and he told me I could stop pushing now. Across the street was a bar, and we went in. I do not remember how he got down to the street, over the sidewalk's curb. He did it alone and we crossed the street and he went over the curb in front of the bar. His crippling came from polio, while he was in the Army. In rehabilitation, he had learned to lean his chair backward, bring the small front wheels down on the curb, and push and lift the big rear wheels onto it.

He had broad shoulders and a deep voice, and I loved hearing it. I do not remember how much of his lower body was paralyzed. He had a girlfriend and, one evening in a bar, he said to me: "I can have intercourse." I do not remember pulling him up the steps to our house when he came for dinner or a party, but we had more than one step, so my wife and I must have helped him. He told me of learning to use a wheelchair, of the instructors taking the men on wheels out of the hospital, racing to a bar. "You had to keep up and get over the curbs," he said. "If you fell on your back, tough shit." He laughed and I laughed with him, and that is how I thought of people in wheelchairs until I became one: stouthearted folk wheeling fast on sidewalks, climbing curbs, and, of course, sometimes falling backward, but that seemed to me like slipping and falling on the outfield grass while chasing a fly ball, until over twenty years later, when I fell backward in my chair, and the quick arc of the fall slammed my head against the floor, and I lay helpless and hurt. It was summer and the windows were open and my neighbor, in his house thirty yards away, heard my head striking wood.

My friend was very skillful in his wheelchair, and I lacked imagination. Or I lacked the compassion and courage to imagine someone else's suffering. I never thought of my friend making his bed, sitting on a toilet, sitting in a shower, dressing himself, preparing breakfast and washing its dishes, just to leave the house, to go out into the freezing air of Iowa.

In my freshman year of college in Louisiana, I studied journalism. If I had become a reporter, and if one day I had walked into a hospital and interviewed a quadriplegic, I would have written the same kind of story I read in the newspaper that November morning. It is a good story. The human spirit is strong, and its strength goes out of a person, and into others. And the heart is capable of such hope that even when we know the truth and it is not the truth we want, we still hope. Probably

I have read Styron's *Lie Down in Darkness* ten times, yet each time Peyton climbs the stairs to leap, I hope she will not. We should celebrate this. I would have, as a reporter; and that night, after writing my story about the brave and hopeful quadriplegic, I would have climbed four steps to a restaurant, eaten dinner with a woman who aroused my functional cock, walked into the men's room and stood pissing in the urinal, and I would not have imagined sitting in a two-hundred-and-fifty-pound wheelchair and looking at those few steps leading to the restaurant's door; or looking into a woman's eyes and, in my chest, feeling passion my body could no longer release.

After the Gulf War, I watched the televised games of the Boston Red Sox. Between innings are commercials, and usually I change channels and watch a movie till the pitcher walks to the mound. But one Saturday afternoon, I saw a commercial: a series of war monuments, and stirring music and a man's voice talking about valor. I saw the Iwo Jima monument, the Marines raising the flag. I was a Marine, between wars. On my couch, watching sculpted brave men in uniforms of different wars, I felt honor and pride. Tears were in my eyes. The Vietnam Veterans Memorial was not in the commercial. I still did not know what the commercial was for; it could have been for recruitment. It could simply have been about America. Then the monuments were gone and what filled the screen was a bottle of Budweiser. Drops of condensation were on the bottle.

I wanted a Budweiser bottle then, to throw at my television screen. But it is my television set, and it gives me pleasure and peace, with baseball games and movies, rarely anything else. I had watched some bombings during the Gulf War, had felt the thrill of killing and winning. So I stopped watching. Now I watched a baseball game and wanted to yell with rage at every human being involved with that commercial, and I thought of Jeannie, a young woman who was an Army lieutenant in the Gulf War. She was born while her father was a Marine lieutenant in Vietnam. Her younger sister, Lynda, worked for me, cleaning my house and helping me with my younger daughters, and she was with us on the night the war started. When we heard that it had begun, my girls and Lynda cried, and all through the war we worried about Jeannie. The day after the war ended, I drove my youngest girl from play school to my house. She is Madeleine, and was four then. I looked back at her in the car seat and said: "The war is over."

"Jeannie will come *home*," she said. "When I see her face, she will look different."

On a warm day in spring, my girls and I saw Jeannie. We went on a picnic with her and Lynda. While Lynda and the girls were playing on the grass in the park, Jeannie said to me: "I'm older. I asked my father when it would go away, and he said: 'It doesn't. This is it.' "

It was the dead, she told me; seeing and smelling the Iraqi soldiers of a bombed convoy. I remembered her father telling me of burying the North Vietnamese dead at Hue, and how sad he was.

Watching the baseball game, I thought of another friend who was a Marine lieutenant in Vietnam, and who was blown into the air by a mine and lost his left leg below the knee. He had been a quarterback in school. When he came home to his small town, limping on an artificial leg, he saw his coach. The coach asked what had happened to his leg, and my friend said: "I twisted my knee."

I met him nearly twenty years after his wounding, and less than a month before a car hit me. We were at a writers' conference, and he did not limp, and when he told me about his leg, I said: "I never would have known." A long time after my injury, when I was still working with a physical therapist, walking on an artificial leg, I talked with this friend on the phone, and reminded him of what I had said that summer, while I walked on my legs and he walked on one of his. He said: "You pissed me off. People don't know how tiring it is, and how much it hurts."

We were talking on the phone again when he told me about his coach. I said: "You didn't tell him you were in the war?"

"I was afraid of his reaction."

*

I did not like writing news stories, and in my second year of college I changed my major to English. In my freshman year, a sportswriter in his forties came to a journalism class and talked to us about his life as a newspaperman. I liked him. He was friendly and good-humored, and cheer was in his eyes. A few years earlier, he had written about the professional baseball games in Louisiana's Class C Evangeline League. One night, because of successive nights of rain, then doubleheaders, a team had no one who could pitch. The league president allowed the sportswriter to pitch; as a young man, he had been a pitcher, a left-hander. That night, he gave up a lot of runs, and the fans and ballplayers were merry; he pitched for nine innings.

In the classroom, he told us that, like all old newspapermen, he had a novel in a trunk. I imagined the life ahead of me, as a reporter, a columnist, an adventurous life that would support me while I wrote fiction, and I believed my manuscripts would not live in a trunk. I wanted to be out of college, in the midst of the challenge. He spoke with encouragement, with acceptance, with passion. His last line, just before the bell, was: "Remember: the last four letters of American spell *I can.*"

My heart filled; tears were in my eyes.

Someone sent me a clipping from the *Wall Street Journal:* a story about a wheelchair that climbs stairs. Computers are involved. The chair has wheels, but you press something, if you are able to press something, and the chair has tracks, and up the stairs you go. There was a picture of the president of the company that made this chair, and the story quoted him: "This is the American way: independence."

The chair costs twenty-eight thousand dollars.

I sing of those who cannot. To view human suffering as an abstraction, as a statement about how plucky we all are, is to blow air through brass while the boys and girls march in parade off to war. Seeing the flesh as only a challenge to the spirit is as false as seeing the spirit as only a challenge to the flesh. On the planet are people with whole and strong bodies, whose wounded spirits need the constant help that the quadriplegic needs for his body. What we need is not the sound of horns rising to the sky, but the steady beat of the bass drum. When you march to a bass drum, your left foot touches the earth with each beat, and you can feel the drum in your body: *boom* and *boom* and *boom* and *pity people pity people pity people*.

Communion

FOR AUSTIN

ONE OF THE MEN WITH CHRIST IN THE Garden of Olives ran away naked. When the crowd came, they grabbed this man too; he was wearing only a linen cloth wrapped around him; they held it and he ran out of it, into the night. This is in the Gospel of Mark. We do not know who he was; so he entered history and remains in it as a man running naked in the dark. Maybe he was not at the Last Supper, but joined Christ and the eleven as they walked to the garden. But imagine him at the Last Supper, one of the first people to receive the Eucharist. He knows in the way Christ's hands hold the bread and wine, and in the way He speaks about them, that something is happening;

he is not certain of what it is. The bread and wine are familiar; he eats, drinks. After the meal, he sings hymns with the others, and Christ. He feels peaceful: understood and loved. They walk to the garden, where he sits on the ground. Then he lies on it, looks up at trees and stars. His stomach is full and soon he is asleep. The noise of men wakes him; then someone is holding him, and he runs naked in the night air, which he wants to keep breathing. He will do anything to be able to breathe, and when he runs far enough, he feels grateful, then ashamed. Now he walks, gaining his breath, and he feels alone; but he is not. He is us.

Maybe a few days later, he walks with a friend on a dusty road from Jerusalem to Emmaus. Christ has been crucified and buried. Now the women say they have seen Him alive, they have embraced His legs and feet, and Mary Magdalene says He spoke to her and she spoke to Him. His tomb is empty. Peter and John have seen it. The man who ran and his friend are sad, confused, afraid. On the road, a man joins them, walks with them, and asks why they are troubled. The two are surprised. Where has this man been? How could he not know what has happened in Jerusalem? Their faith and hope and love have been broken and scattered there, and now pieces of them are returning, as though on the wind, in the voices of the women who saw Him alive, and the men who saw the empty tomb. But what can they do with these pieces? On the road, they tell all of this to the man who has joined

them, and He says: "Don't you understand?" Then
He teaches them the Scriptures they already know,
the words that predicted Christ's coming. They
reach Emmaus and invite their companion for a
meal at an inn. At a wooden table, He sits opposite
them. A young woman brings a basket of bread; He
blesses the bread, and breaks it, and hands pieces
to them. Then they see that He is Christ, and He
vanishes. Now they know what they were feeling,
walking on the road, and the man who ran says:
"Weren't our hearts burning? When He talked to
us, on the road?" Later, the Holy Spirit will come in
flames to the gathered disciples, and the church
will move over the earth, in the voices of men and
women and children, in their flesh.

Or maybe the man who ran is with Peter on a
boat at night. Christ is dead and life goes on and
they are trying to catch fish. From the shore at
dawn, a man calls to them, tells them to fish on the
other side of the boat; John says: "It's the Lord,"
and Peter swims ashore where Christ waits with fish
He has cooked over coals, and with bread. He eats
with them. Or the man is one of those in a crowded
room, and suddenly Christ is there, showing His
wounds, and talking to them, and they give Him
fish to eat.

Christ kept eating with people after He was
dead. He still does. The Last Supper is not in the
past, but in the present. *Before Abraham was, I am*
means the time and mortality the man ran naked
for and from are real, and are to be feared and

loved; but that before time and mortality, God is, and so love is; and God's love entered them and mortality as a baby, a boy, a man, to show itself through the flesh. Knowing that those few years of physical presence are not enough, He remains in the flesh: in bread and wine, in the acts of eating and drinking. The Communion with God is simple, so we will not be dazzled; so we can eat and drink His love and still go about our lives; so our souls will burn slowly rather than blaze.

We can live with this miracle, for it requires so little of our bodies and minds and hearts. We simply have to be where the Eucharist is, and open our mouths to it. We can even receive it without eating it. On most mornings after my accident, I did not have the energy to go to Mass, then prepare meals and write and try alone to run a household. A priest brought me the Eucharist when he had time to, and once he said: "Every day you are receiving Communion of desire; other people are receiving it for you." So the Last Supper did not take place on one night in one room, and to eat God's love, we do not even have to open our mouths; we can be walking, sorrowful and confused, with a friend; or working on whatever our boat is, fishing for whatever it is we fish for; we can be running naked, alone in the dark. The Eucharist is with us, and it is ordinary. To me, that is its essential beauty: we receive it with wandering minds, and distracted flesh, in the same way that we receive the sun and sky, the moon and earth, and breathing.

First Books

MY FIRST BOOK WAS A NOVEL, BOUGHT by Dial Press when I was twenty-nine, and published when I was thirty. If I were a young writer now, thirty years later, that book would not be published. My first book would be the collection of stories that was my second book, published when I was thirty-nine, in 1975, by David R. Godine, a small publisher. In 1975, Mark Smith, the novelist, told me that the average age of the writer of a first novel or book of stories would from then on be thirty-nine. He said publishers used to buy a writer's talent, hoping that the writer's fourth or fifth book would sell enough copies to earn money. He said:

"Now they want the money with the first book." When Dial bought my novel, they were doing what publishers used to do: paying a small advance, printing a small number of books, and waiting for me to grow, or my readers to multiply. They did not want my second book, because it was a collection of stories, and years later, with gratitude, I found David Godine.

I am writing this over twenty years after Mark Smith's prediction. In this decade, I have read manuscripts of good novels and collections of stories that New York publishers have rejected. These rejections are not the sort that should dishearten a writer; in essence, they have said: I like this book, but I don't know how to sell it. One day a couple of years ago, my concern shifted for a few moments from writers to editors, and I phoned my agent and told him there must be a lot of frustrated editors too. He said: Of course there are; an editor wants to buy a book and he shows it to the editor in chief, who talks to the sales force, and one of those people calls someone at the bookstore chains, a guy who was selling cars six months ago and thinks of a book as a *unit*, and that guy says, We won't sell it, and the editor has to reject it. I do not know if Mark Smith was thinking about bookstore chains in 1975, or if now they are the major reason for large publishing houses' treatment of first books. But I do know that it is much harder now to publish a first book than it has ever been in my adult life, and I believe the small publishers, always important as the homes of poets, are more important, offering more hope, than ever before.

A first book is a treasure, and all these truths and quasi-truths I have written about publishing are finally ephemeral. An older writer knows what a younger one has not yet learned. What is demanding and fulfilling is writing a single word, trying to write *le mot juste*, as Flaubert said; writing several of them, which become a sentence. When a writer does that, day after day, working alone with little encouragement, often with discouragement flowing in the writer's own blood, and with an occasional rush of excitement that empties oneself, so that the self is for minutes longer in harmony with eternal astonishments and visions of truth, right there on the page on the desk, and when a writer does this work steadily enough to complete a manuscript long enough to be a book, the treasure is on the desk. If the manuscript itself, mailed out to the world, where other truths prevail, is never published, the writer will suffer bitterness, sorrow, anger, and, more dangerously, despair, convinced that the work is not worthy, so not worth those days at the desk. But the writer who endures and keeps working will finally know that writing the book was something hard and glorious, for at the desk a writer must try to be free of prejudice, meanness of spirit, pettiness, and hatred; strive to be a better human being than the writer normally is, and to do this through concentration on a single word, and then another, and another. This is splendid work, as worthy and demanding as any, and the will and resilience to do it are good for the writer's soul. If the work is not published, or is published for little money and less public attention, it remains a spiritual, mental, and physical achievement; and if, in public, it is the widow's mite, it is also, like the widow, more blessed.

Letter to Amtrak

This was before the Americans with Disabilities Act. That act would not have helped me on the train, but it would have prevented American Airlines' attempt to keep me off a plane. Only Senator Edward Kennedy answered my letter; he also wrote to the Department of Transportation, and a man from the Department contacted me and said he could get me on any plane I chose, but he could do nothing about airlines charging for a first-class ticket, though I had no other choice but to sit in the front seat. Amtrak sent me a form letter dealing with inconvenienced customers; the letter constituted a gift certificate for a sum I don't recall, except that it was under a hundred dollars. Amtrak wrote to Kennedy, or the Depart-

*ment of Transportation—I forget which—and said the
toilet in that compartment was accessible. My friend Jack
Herlihy, who traveled with me, got me onto the toilet. He
told me to put my leg and stump over the left wheel. Then
he dragged the chair sideways to the toilet, the right wheel
against its front, and I backed over that wheel and lowered myself to the toilet. Then Jack pulled the chair away,
to make room for my leg, and went to his room across the
passageway, leaving me with the shards of my privacy.*

I AM SITTING IN MY WHEELCHAIR, TWO DAYS
before the Fourth of July, trying for the third
time in four months to write to you of the emo-
tional pain and humiliation of my experience as an
Amtrak passenger on 10 March 1990. I am enclosing a copy of the letter by Amtrak Chief-on-Board
Sheila Beyda-McGraw. I have taken so long to write
to you because it hurts me to write about it. I had
an overnight berth on the train from Albany to
Chicago, and the toilet in the berth, and all toilets
on the train, were inaccessible.

I used to be able to walk, until a car hit me in
1986 and I lost a leg, and the other one received
such severe damage that I am now confined to a
wheelchair. I used to enjoy traveling by Amtrak. In
the winter of 1989, I planned a trip to Seattle and
Portland, so my reservations were nearly a year
in advance when I boarded the train at Boston on
10 March 1990, to travel to Albany and then to

Chicago. In Boston, the door to the coach for handicapped people, a door with a wheelchair painted on it, would not open widely enough for my chair to go through it. With some hard work, my oldest son, my traveling companion, and Amtrak personnel got me into another coach, the club car. Then at Albany, I changed trains and was in a berth with a toilet I could not use.

I am a fifty-three-year-old writer, a father of six children, a former Marine officer, a voter, a taxpayer, an American *citizen*, and from Boston, Massachusetts, until I boarded a train in Chicago, Illinois, *I could not use a toilet*. As I wheeled my chair into the station at Chicago, I looked up at the large American flag on the wall and for the first time in my life I felt that it did not include me, it did not want me. I felt not like a man or a father, but a damaged piece of meat. On the return trip, we flew from Chicago to Boston on American Airlines, which is not American either; they did not want me: they told my travel agent if I did not have a traveling companion, they would not allow me on board; and they made a lot of money because my remaining leg has to be elevated, so I had to be in the front seat, which is of course first class. I believe Amtrak should refund the cost of the trip, for me and my traveling companion, from Boston to Albany.

But that is not why I am writing to you. If I were the only disabled person in this country, we could just call it bad luck and forget about it. There are millions of us and we must have access to trains. I want access to trains. I want to go to Baton Rouge on the New Orleans Crescent in December for a niece's wedding. I want to go to the University of Alabama in September 1991 for a symposium on the short story. Politicians lose something when they travel by air. Do you know what happens when you travel by train? You see the country the way you saw it as a child, in history and geography classes. Once, when I could walk, and therefore had the right to use a bathroom, I traveled from New York to San Francisco. I woke the first morning in the flat fields of the Midwest, the train cutting through them as if this were a hundred years ago; then out the window appeared the skyline of Chicago, a huge sculpted city rising out of the earth, and if you're traveling by train instead of by air, you suddenly see the history, feel it. Ah, the water, you think. It started with water that led to the sea; they built wharves and warehouses and saloons and dry-goods stores. You see things like that, on the train; and you see where the poor live, because always the tracks go through where the poor live; you see things like the juxtaposition of homes along the tracks in Philadelphia and then Bryn Mawr; you see antelope grazing in Wyoming. You can cross the nation from sea to shining sea.

But if you're in a wheelchair, you can't use a bathroom east of Chicago. If those conditions of bladder and bowels had been imposed on the settlers of this country, they wouldn't have gotten as far as Albany. In Albany on the night of 10 March, the Amtrak people at the station were unkind. They had a simple and curt attitude: It's your problem; you can stay on the train or get off. So I stayed. What would I do in Albany? I wanted them to fly me and my friend to Chicago to catch the train next day. No guarantee, they said; you can take your chances, they said; this train is leaving. Car attendant Barrick Ketchum was particularly kind and showed great empathy from Albany to Chicago. Sheila Beyda-McGraw was as compassionate as a human being can be.

I'm sending copies of this to several of our leaders. I want them and you to get to work and make American citizens of those of us who are handicapped; I want us to be citizens wherever we travel in this country, whose anniversary is this week. We'd like to be able to walk, but we can't. There's nothing we can do about that. You've got to do that for us, the way our friends do, those of us who have friends. Some of us don't, and you certainly can't travel alone in a wheelchair on Amtrak. But you don't travel alone either. Nobody does. We either buy help or receive it from people who love us, or both; and those who are truly alone die, in the spirit and in the flesh. Give spirit to our flesh; give our flesh a private place where we can sit on a toilet, then return down wide aisles to our coaches or berths to look out windows at the vast stretch and climb of America; let us bring our particular and private suffering to a train that is truly public and open to all who have the price of a ticket, all races and beliefs, all manner of broken and diseased bodies. Let us gather in dignity and kindness and grace; let us be Americans on your trains too; let us see our country.

cc: President George Bush,
Barbara Bush,
Sen. Edward Kennedy,
Sen. John Kerry

Autumn Legs

IN MY DREAMS, I AM NEVER IN THE WHEEL-
chair. Usually, I have legs, and at times I have the
stump and somehow walk with my one damaged
leg. One afternoon, on the first day of autumn, I
lay clothed on my bed and slept, and dreamed I
was driving on a sunlit and warm afternoon. My
golden retriever, Luke, was in the car. I was driving
southeast toward the sea, on a two-lane asphalt
road through rolling country with trees and meadows. I could sense the Atlantic to my left, beyond
the hills. There was no one else on the road. I did
not know where I was going, or why, or how I would
know when I got there; but I knew I was driving to

a place. The road dipped and wound between trees, then flattened, and on my left was a green field. Beside it was an asphalt parking space and I turned into it and parked vertically and, with Luke, got out of the car.

We went into the field. Luke was very old and slow then. The grass was above my ankles, and I started to run; Luke ran beside me, and now he was leaner, young and quick. Then I saw that I was too: I was running smoothly, wearing burgundy slacks I had worn in my thirties. We started up a long slope with high grass, and we were breathing easily, and suddenly I knew I was dead. Imagine this: you have a one-year-old child; you are driving alone in your car, on a highway, and your home is thirty minutes behind you. Then all at once your breath and heart quicken, and a chill rises from your stomach to your heart and spreads: you have left home without your child, you did not mean to, but this is what you have done, and the child is alone and must have you now and you must be there now, in this quivering instant of loss so bright that you do not even see the road, the hills flanking it, the blue sky; you see only the child crawling on the floor and the great distance between your back and the child you have left behind to hunger and thirst, to be alone, to be afraid, to be taken by a madman, to die in the burning house. You must find an exit, and make your way back to the highway going home, and you must do this faster than it can possibly be

done; you want to do it all at once, will yourself
back to your child, with no intervals of time and
space.

It was like that. I kept running. The slope curved
to the right and I saw trees and low brick buildings
in their shade. Luke and I ran to the top of the hill
and slowed to a walk at the trees. A man stood
ahead of us; he wore a gray suit and a tie, and he
smiled pleasantly, as though he knew me. I stopped
and said to him: "Am I dead?"

He nodded.

"No," I said. "I can't. I've got two little girls."

"You can see them."

I followed him into the building on our left, and
Luke stayed near the trees. The man and I walked
down a cool and dim and very clean hall to a large
room that was also dim and clean, where children
played on the carpeted floor or sat in leather
couches and chairs, watching television. They were
the ages of my girls. There were no adults, and not
all the children knew one another, but they
seemed cared for, and they were content and
patient. Soon parents would come and take them
home. Then I saw Madeleine and Cadence. Madeleine was two, and she was playing on the floor with
other children; she was facing me, but looking
down at toys. Cadence was seven. She was sitting on
a leather couch with other girls, watching television, her face in profile to me. Madeleine looked
up and saw me, and stood and walked toward me,
and I said: "I knew you'd be able to see me."

Then Cadence turned to me and said: "I saw you."

I was no longer desperate to get back. I grieved because I could not; then I woke grieving and quickly left the bed, and got onto my chair. I wheeled down the hall, remembering Swedenborg's visions of heaven, where we become angels, where I would have both legs, and they would be young and strong. The sadness I fled from in my chair stayed with me in the early days of autumn. Now I write this on an afternoon in May, and lilacs are in a vase on my desk, and beyond the glass door in front of me young maples are bright green in the sun. Yesterday, Cadence picked the lilacs for me.

Giving Up the Gun

IN THE WINTER OF 1990, SITTING IN MY wheelchair in a sleeping compartment on a train from Portland, Oregon, to Chicago, I gave up my guns and the protection I believed they gave people I loved, and strangers whose peril I might witness, and me. At home in Massachusetts, I had a metal gun box with two locks, and in it were eight handguns, one a small twenty-two-caliber revolver that is four and a half inches long. In my wallet on the train, I had a Massachusetts license to carry firearms. In the space on the card for occupation, a police officer had typed *Author;* in the space under *Reason for Issuing License,* he had typed *Protection.*

For thirteen years, I had a license, renewing it every five years. I still have the one that was with me on the train, but it expired four years ago, in 1991, and the guns have been locked in their box since I returned from Oregon. Thirteen years before I rode that train, someone I love was raped in Boston by a man who held a knife at her throat. I went to my local police chief and told him I wanted a license, and that my father had taught me to shoot, and the Marine Corps had, and I would safely own a gun, and no woman would ever be raped if I were with her. I cursed and wept and he was sympathetic and said he would immediately start the background investigation by the state. A detective made a rolled impression of my right index finger, and I went to a photographer for a picture.

In about three weeks, I had my license and I went to a sporting-goods store to choose and buy a gun: a Charter Arms thirty-eight-caliber snubnosed revolver, because it cost less than a Smith & Wesson or a Colt. I did not own a suit and rarely wore a sport coat, so a shoulder holster would not do. The store owner made me a shadow holster: a leather one whose belt slot was low, so that most of the holster and the gun were above my waist. I could wear a pullover shirt, or sweater, or even a loose-fitting T-shirt, and you could not see the gun. So my thirteen years as an armed man began.

For a long time, I put the gun on my belt only when I went to Boston with a woman. Then I was certain that she was safe, and I was also certain that

I would never have to use the gun; that simply being prepared for rapists or other violent men would keep them from my path. And if that failed, I was certain that I would not have to shoot anyone; I would only have to hold the gun in my hand and point it at a man while the woman with me called the police. Maybe I would have to fire a shot straight up in the air, if this man I did not believe would be part of my life appeared anyway, intent on removing me with his fists or a weapon, and taking the woman. If a shot in the air did not change his dark direction and send him running, if instead he attacked, I would shoot his leg or shoulder. This was all very tidy, and I believed it.

After a few years, and a lot of newspaper stories, I began asking myself questions whose answers were not in my brain, my body, my gun, but in my soul, though I did not know that. What if I went with a man to watch the Red Sox or a movie, and we saw several men or one big one attacking a woman or a man, not to steal, but to harm or rape or kill? I was no hand-to-hand fighter, and did not intend to be. I also did not intend to watch a crucifixion in any form. I started bringing a gun every time I went to Boston: to Fenway Park, to jazz clubs, to dinner in restaurants, to movies.

When I fired the Charter Arms thirty-eight at a target, it often spit tiny fragments of lead toward my face. I sold it at a gun store and bought a used three-eighty semiautomatic, which looks like a

very small forty-five, and I put it in the pocket of
my jeans, with my keys and coins, and it was flat
enough to be concealed. Through the years, when
I had the money, I bought other guns. One was a
Smith & Wesson snub-nosed thirty-eight that fit in
the shadow holster. By now, I had begun loading
guns with hollow-point bullets, so if I had to shoot
a human being in the shoulder or leg, the bullet
would not go through him and hit someone else; it
would shatter into pieces inside his body. The guns
were to protect other people. No one would rape
me. If someone wanted my money, he could have
it. If someone felt like beating me, I could run. But
I had the gun, and I believed that nothing would
happen, simply because I was prepared for it; and
that if something did happen, it would be as I had
imagined it. My confidence in this was foolish, and
the foolishness was as concealed from my soul as
the gun in my pocket or holster was concealed
from the eyes of other people.

Alabama has stricter handgun laws than Massachusetts, or it did in 1985, when I went by train
with my wife and our three-year-old daughter, and
brought guns for hunting, target shooting, and to
put in my pocket or in a holster under my coat, if I
felt I needed it in Tuscaloosa. I went there to earn
money, to hold the writing chair for a semester at
the University of Alabama. Because I grew up in
Louisiana, where guns in homes were ordinary,

where an adult could carry a gun if it was not concealed, and men who worked in woods or swamps often wore holstered handguns so they could shoot snakes, I assumed that Alabama in 1985 would be like Louisiana in the forties and fifties. A few days after we moved into the large and free house that came with the job in Tuscaloosa, I went to the sheriff's office and showed a deputy my Massachusetts permit, and asked him if I could carry a handgun. He said that no one could carry a handgun in Alabama; that a resident, after a background investigation, could buy one and take it home but could not take it out of the home. The deputy was a friendly man, and after we talked for a while, he told me to get a letter from the English department, showing that I was employed in Alabama. He said the letter and my Massachusetts license would make everything all right.

"If it went to court," he said, "the judge would throw it out."

"What if there's trouble, and I have to use it?"

"Then it's never a problem."

Tuscaloosa did not feel like a place where I needed a gun. Of course if you feel the need to carry a gun, you need one everywhere. But the territory of violence was in my imagination: cities were places where predators lived; towns and small cities were not. Unarmed, I drove and walked in Tuscaloosa, until I bought the four-and-a-half-inch-long twenty-two revolver, stainless steel, with brown plastic handgrips. It holds five rounds, and you load and unload it by removing the cylinder, which means the gun is as safe as a handgun can be: the cylinder is either in place or it is not; and if it is, you handle the gun as though it is loaded, even when you know it is not. Because of the training given me by my father and the Marine Corps, I always assume a gun is loaded. I also attribute to a gun the ability to load itself, even fire itself, without being touched by a human hand.

I love guns, especially well-made pistols and revolvers. Many of them are beautiful, and their shape and balanced weight are pleasing to hold. I love the relaxed concentration of aiming a gun and squeezing its trigger, the thrill of hitting a bull's-eye or a can. When I hold a gun, I do not imagine the death of a human being, which is the purpose of most handguns. I know people who are frightened or appalled by guns and do not want to hold one, spin its cylinder or pull its slide to the rear and watch and hear it move forward, hear that perfect and final click as the slide pushes a bullet into the chamber. These people are right: they see a bullet entering a human body. In the gun store in Alabama, I held the tiny twenty-two as another person might hold a pocket watch or a ring, a hammer or a golf club. To me, that gun, like all my guns, was somehow alive, with a history and a future; with a soul. I loved it, and bought it.

Before I could take it home, I had to wait about a week for permission from the state of Alabama. At home, I took out the cylinder, loaded it with four rounds of hollow-points, leaving an empty chamber under the hammer, and put the gun in the right pocket of my jeans, with my coins, keys, and lighter, and it was always there, when I left the house for Mass or work, errands or shopping, or pleasure. I had not fired it, and did not expect to until I went home to Massachusetts, where in my basement I had a target for twenty-two-caliber weapons. The little gun in my pocket amused me. It was, I said, for gentle places, where there would be no trouble. I called it "Misty."

If it had not been in my pocket the night I aimed it at a man's stomach, I do not know what would have happened on that crowded sidewalk across the street from the university. The night was a Friday, my wife and daughter were out of town, visiting relatives in the North, the evening was warm, and I began it with happy hour on the patio of a restaurant we writers liked. Most of the writers I knew were graduate students, and we liked this place because we could drink cheaply and afford Mexican appetizers until six o'clock. One of the women that evening on the patio was a graduate student who was separated from her husband, and had a young daughter she was afraid would live with the father. Later, she and her husband lived together and remained married, but that night it did not seem possible, and she was in pain.

She had driven me to the bar, and at six o'clock, when the prices of drinks changed and the writers dispersed and went to other cheap bars or home for dinner, the woman and I drove to a video store. We had decided while drinking that we wanted to watch *Rebel Without a Cause*. We rented it to watch at my house, but we wanted first to sit in a quiet air-conditioned bar and drink club sodas and talk about divorce, and she drove there; it was twilight now and the streetlamps were on. She parked around the corner from a block of bars and restaurants facing the campus. We walked to the corner. Then a man with no hands came around it and stopped in front of me. He was stocky and short, and I looked down at his face. I was taking a cigarette from a pack when he asked me for money. I offered him a cigarette; I did not know how he would smoke it, but I felt that he did not want my help. Somehow, with his stumps or an elbow, he got it to his lips. I was not watching; I was taking money from my wallet and slipping it into the left pocket of his pants. Then I gave him a light. He said: "I saw that."

I do not remember what he did with the cigarette. I said: "You can buy me a drink."

"Where?"

I nodded at the bar beside us. He said: "I can't go in there."

"Why?"

"I'm eighty-sixed."

"Let's go anyway."

The three of us went inside; it was crowded with students, and dark, with loud talk and laughter and music from the jukebox, and I went to the bar. The bartender was a young man. He said: "Sir, that man can't come in here."

"Why?"

"He makes trouble."

I wondered what kind of trouble a man with no hands could make. We went outside. The man without hands said: "Let's go to my place."

"No thanks; we're going down the street."

He crossed the street to a liquor store on the opposite corner, and the woman and I watched. He came out with a case of beer on his right shoulder, his stump holding it in place. He lifted the other to wave, and we waved at him. Then a young blond man was standing with us; he had come out of the bar. He looked like an undergraduate. He said: "Mister, that man is trouble."

"What can he do, without hands?"

"Believe me, he's trouble."

He was an affable young man, and the three of us chatted for a while. He invited us to have a drink, but we thanked him and walked down the block to a well-lighted bar where you could nearly always sit among quiet strangers. We did that, and drank club sodas with wedges of lime and dashes of bitters, and talked about divorce. We assumed her daughter would not live with her. I had never known a woman who had lost custody of her child, but I knew her pain. We talked about it and drank club sodas for two hours or more, and I no longer felt the happy-hour margaritas. While we were becoming sober, the young blond man, in the bar at the corner, was probably drinking too much. It is easy to conclude that someone dangerous at night, outside of a bar, is drunk; but I shall never know whether that man was drunk and was doing something he would not want to do in his normal state, or was a violent man whose trajectory met mine on a sidewalk in Alabama.

When the woman and I left our seats at the bar, I was tired because of what we had talked about, and neither of us was certain we still wanted to watch the movie. Deciding to see it had been delightful when the sun was shining and we were drinking in its light on the patio. Now it was nearly ten o'clock. We stepped out of the air-conditioned bar, into the warm air and streetlights, and I held her elbow, guiding her through a group of large black men who had come down a stairway from an upstairs bar. I felt her body tense, and I looked at her face. She looked afraid. I do not know why. In Alabama, except for that Friday night, I saw no trouble between white and black people, and I did not hear any bigotry. This was one of many reasons I loved my time there.

When I left Louisiana in the spring of 1958, integration was inchoate. In my sophomore year of college, black students had enrolled. In the student union, they sat with one another; I do not remember any black men playing on a varsity team. I grew up feeling compassion for black people; you could not live in a segregated town, even as a young boy, and not see injustice. I also felt involved in this injustice, and stained by it; I still do. I did not want black people to drink at different public water fountains, go into different public bathrooms, sit in the balcony of one movie theater (they could not go into our other two theaters); I did not want them to ride on the back of the bus, but they did, and there I was at the front of the bus, even if black people had to stand in its crowded rear. And my parents had taught me, their only son, always to offer my seat to a woman. I did not want black people to live in their part of town, with its dirt roads and hovels. I did not want them to be subservient, and their work to be menial, but they were and it was; and I grew and learned and played in the sun.

This was in Lafayette, Louisiana, a small city then, and I do not remember any violence engendered by black boys or men. Nor do I remember white boys or men assaulting black people. As I write this in 1995, black people in America are still beyond the pale; white people have created and maintained ghettos where understandable hopelessness and rage keep true freedom of the body and spirit at bay. It is a world I was born to skirt, for I am white, and it is a world I can avoid by simply having enough money to buy a house on an acre and a quarter of land in Massachusetts. I would not wheel about in my chair in a ghetto, because I am afraid; and I am afraid because I believe that only God's grace can keep many black people from feeling anger about anyone who is white; and we often turn away from God's grace; or His voice is lost in the clamor of simply being alive.

In Lafayette in the forties and fifties, we were not afraid of black people. Some of us—I think most of us—were respectful, some were scornful, some were hateful. I doubt that any of us, boys and girls, men and women, felt that we and black people were equal, despite what our priests told us. How can you feel equal, save in the heart of God, with someone who is always excluded? I believe I saw no violence between white and black boys because we were never with one another in schools, or on playgrounds, or in swimming pools, or even in groups on the street or, as we grew older, in bars and nightclubs; and I believe also that black people were afraid of us. Many of them moved among us with the caution of wild birds. In my boyhood, there were no lynchings in Louisiana; or I do not remember any. But how could any black person in the segregated South not be aware of this horror?

In Tuscaloosa in 1985, black people were everywhere, in the stores, on the sidewalks, on the campus and in classrooms, in bars and theaters and churches. I do not know why the woman seemed afraid as we strolled through the group of black men, standing happily at ease on a hot night. She and I walked nearly the length of the block, were at the corner where we had talked with the man without hands and the young blond man, when I heard a man's voice say: "Nigger."

I stopped and turned. The young blond man stood about twenty-five feet from me, in front of the plate-glass window of a restaurant; in his right hand was an open pocketknife with a long and wide blade, and he was looking at a small black man. Behind the black man was a wall, and his back touched it. The blond man slowly moved toward him. I put my right hand in the pocket of my jeans, gripped the revolver and pulled it out and cocked it and aimed it at the blond man's stomach. I knew nothing about the accuracy of this little gun; if I fired at his shoulder or leg, I might not hit him at all. I saw the gun sight at the front of the barrel, his stomach, the silver blade of his knife, and his face. To his right, some young white men were telling him not to do this; but to me, they were as distant as campus buildings hundreds of yards away. I still do not know how many of them stood there. My hand aiming the gun was steady and I said loudly: "Put away the knife."

He looked at me, recognized me, and said: "Fuck you."

I had no images of my history or my future, not even of pulling the trigger or not pulling the trigger. The voices of his friends, indeed all sounds on the sidewalk and street and coming from the bar on the corner, only a few feet to my right, were like wind you have been hearing for hours. All of me focused on the knife; it had to disappear; and I was mysteriously calm. I said: "Put it back in your pocket, or I'll shoot."

"Fuck you." He was not moving. I glanced at the black man, standing against the wall. The woman stood to my left; either she was silent or I did not hear her; she too was as distant from me as everyone else on the sidewalk, save the blond man and the black man at the wall. I remember only one instant of one wish: that the black man would run away. I said: "I mean it."

He spread his arms from his body, and said: "Fuck you. Shoot. Go ahead. Shoot."

The voices of his friends rose, I could see their hands and faces to his right, and they were pleading with him; but they did not touch him. By now, probably the group of black men the woman and I had walked through had gathered, watching us; I did not see them; but when it ended, they were standing near us. The young man's arms were still spread, and he said: "Shoot me. Go ahead. Shoot me."

Over the barrel of the gun, I looked at his stomach; my arm was extended; the gun was steady. I said: "It's a twenty-two hollow-point, son. It'll spread your guts all over that window."

"All right." He started walking toward me, his friends on his right moving with him, talking to him. Then he was close to me, and everything had changed. I pointed the gun in the air, held its hammer with my thumb, gently squeezed the trigger, and lowered the hammer into place. Then I held the gun at my side. He still held the knife; when he was two feet from me, he stopped and said: "Tell you what. I'll give my buddy the knife, and you give her the gun, and you and me'll fight it out."

I imagined the back of my head hitting the sidewalk. He was young and he looked strong and he would knock me down and the concrete would fracture my skull and I would die here. I said: "I don't want to fight."

I do not remember the sentence he spoke then, only the word *nigger;* then all I felt was resignation. I would have to fight him, receive whatever pain and injury he dealt, until someone stopped him, or he was done with me. I was not angry; I felt nothing about him.

"That's it," I said, and I dropped the revolver into the woman's large purse. Then one of his friends stood between us, his face close to mine, and said: "Mister, I know you can whip his ass. But please leave. I've got to get him out of here before the cops come."

"Okay," I said, and held the woman's elbow and walked away, around the corner. We stopped, and I took the gun from her purse. Then a cruiser came onto the street of bars, quietly, but with flashing lights, and I looked around the corner and watched it stop; two police officers got out and walked to the young blond man. The woman and I went to her car and, as she started it, I said: "Men are funny. If that guy had said: 'I know he can whip *your* ass,' I would have had to fight him. But he said: 'You can whip his ass.' So he let me off the hook."

Then she was trembling.

"Violence scares me," she said. "I have to go home."

"Me too."

She drove me there, and I took the video, to return it to the store, and went inside and filled a glass with ice and took it and a Coke to the front porch. I sat on the steps in the warm night and looked at trees and the sky. I needed the company of women and children; I wanted my wife and daughter to be upstairs, sleeping. I sat for a long time. Saturday morning, I phoned my wife, then a man who was a poet, a hunter, a fisherman, and who lived in the country near Tuscaloosa, and I told him about Friday night, and said I wanted to go out and hunt squirrels with him, to be in the beautiful woods and use a gun the way it ought to be used.

Monday, my wife and daughter were home, and I went to Mass at noon. After Mass, I talked to the young chaplain and a young nun. We stood in front of the chapel, in warm sunlight. The nun was pretty and wore jeans; I always liked seeing her and talking to her; being attracted to a woman and knowing that what we shared was God and my attraction could not become carnal was lovely. I told them about the man and the knife and my gun. I said: "I understand turning the other cheek. But what about turning somebody else's cheek? Christ doesn't say anything about that. What about the woman they were going to stone for adultery? What would He have done if they had picked up rocks and started throwing them at her? It wasn't His time yet. He couldn't stand in front of her and get killed. He had to wait to be crucified. Would He throw rocks at them?" I looked at the priest's eyes, and nodded toward the nun. "What would you do if some guys tried to rape her?"

"I'd fight them."

Still I had no peace. A young man could be dead because of one moment on a Friday night. I did not know what else I could have done but aim my gun at him until either the knife or the black man was gone. I still do not know. I could have kept the gun in my pocket and tried to disarm him. When I was a Marine officer candidate, the sergeant who taught hand-to-hand fighting said: "If someone pulls a knife on you in a bar, run; if you can't run, throw an ashtray or bottle at his face and charge him." Then the sergeant showed us one way to grab the man's wrist, move behind him, and push his arm into a hammerlock. It was a move you would have to practice. I thought about this, during those days and nights in Tuscaloosa, while I kept hoping to know what I should have done. Sometimes, seeing the young man's face, I saw myself trying to grab his wrist, saw his knife piercing my flesh, my aorta. But none of this applied: that night on the sidewalk, my only instinct had been to aim a gun. I had no conflict, because I had only one choice. Now I wanted more choices, and I wanted to know what they were.

At Thanksgiving, my wife and daughter and I rode on the train to Baton Rouge to visit my oldest sister, Kathryn. In the evening, after dinner, people came to Kathryn's house. One was a priest, and one was a nun in her fifties. I imagined the eyes of Christ were like her eyes: in them were strength and depth, and she was cheerful and wise. The priest was in his thirties, short and graceful and athletically built. He lifted weights and had a black belt in karate, and he engaged in contact karate matches. His eyes were like John the Baptist's, or the way I imagined his to be: they were dark and bright with embers that could become rage. He and the nun and I stood with drinks; I felt he would have an answer for me, and I told him my story. He said: "Within the realm of human possibility, you did what you could. You wanted no one to be harmed. And no one was. I beat up a man on Christmas Eve, then said the midnight Mass."

"You did?"

"I was delivering food to the poor. When I got to

his house, he was beating his wife. I took her and the children to another house, then went back to talk to him. Then he tried to beat me."

So I had my answer, and the comfort of it. Within the realm of human possibility, I had done what I could.

I have written all of this to try to discover why, sitting in my wheelchair on a train, I gave up my guns. But I do not know. Eight months after that Thanksgiving in Baton Rouge, I was driving home from Boston, armed with a pistol, and I stopped on the highway and got out of my car to help two people who had driven over an abandoned motorcycle. Then a car hit me, and I have been in a wheelchair for over nine years. My body can no longer do what I want to do, and it cannot protect my two young daughters, and my grandchildren, from perils I used to believe I could save people from. I have not learned the virtue of surrender—which I want— but I have learned the impossibility of avoiding surrender. I am also more afraid now. For the first three years and eight months after my injury, until those moments on the train, I believed I needed a gun more than I ever had. Alone in my house, I kept a small twenty-two Beretta semiautomatic in my shoulder bag, its loaded magazine in one of the bag's pockets, and for the first time in my life, the gun was to protect myself.

I only know this: on the train, images came to

me: I was alone in my house, on the couch, watching a movie on video, and a man kicked my door open and came in, to steal, beat, kill; and I shoved the magazine into the pistol and worked its slide and aimed the gun, but he kept coming at me, and I shot his leg, but he kept coming, and I shot his chest, again and again, till he stopped coming. Then, as I looked out the train window at snow on the ground, one sentence came to me: With my luck, I'll kill someone.

That was all. *Luck* was not the accurate word, and I do not know what the accurate word is. But with that sentence, I felt the fence and gate, not even the lawn and porch and door to the house of sorrow I would live in if I killed someone. Then I felt something detach itself from my soul, departing, rising, vanishing; and I said to God: *It's up to You now.* This is not the humble and pure and absolutely spiritual love of turning the other cheek. It is not an answer to turn someone else's cheek. On the train, I gave up answers that are made of steel that fire lead, and I decided to sit in a wheelchair on the frighteningly invisible palm of God.

Messages

I AM GIVING THEM DIFFERENT NAMES. Late on a Sunday morning in summer, I was on my sundeck, feeling the sun, looking at grass, birds, blue sky, trees. Behind me, the door to the house was open. I heard the telephone ring. I was tense, listening. Everything was beautiful out here in the sun; I did not want to go inside and talk on the telephone. After four rings, the machine answered. I had Sinatra on the tape: he sang a line, then I spoke, then Sinatra sang another line. The caller listened to this for ten or twelve seconds, then talked. I did not know him; he sounded like a workingman, and in his voice were nuances of longing and affection. He said: "Betsy? This is Dave." I turned my wheelchair around and went through the door. "I haven't seen you in a while." I pushed down the hall. "If you'd like to get together, maybe we could meet tonight at that place we like." I turned into the dining room, wheeled toward the kitchen, to the telephone on the wall. "Okay, I hope I see you there." As I passed the telephone, I grabbed it, listened to a dial tone, wished he had left a number.

So she knew his number, or he did not want to be called. It could be adultery or other cheating. But she was not the unfaithful one; he would have hung up when Betsy did not answer. Maybe he was married, or living with a woman, and Betsy shared a place with a man who was neither her husband nor lover, so Dave heard my voice and still spoke to the machine. Maybe erotic love was not an element. But something had been in his voice, and he had not named the place where he wanted to be with her.

Next day at noon, I was on the deck, putting seed in the bird feeder. The phone rang, and I did not move. Then I heard Dave's voice, and I turned and went through the door, calling: "Don't hang up!" He said: "Betsy? This is Dave. I hear you were at that place we like last night, looking for me." I was in the dining room when he said: "I'll go there tonight, maybe you'll be there." I rolled quickly into the kitchen, reaching for the telephone; he hung up. Still I picked up the telephone. He was gone.

But where? Was he at work now? Would he go home after work, to shower and put on clean clothes, eat alone or with his wife, perhaps some children, or with a girlfriend? Then he would go to a bar I had never seen: it was large and dark. He would go there, with hope that was in his voice. Would Betsy be there? I imagined her tonight, in her thirties, wearing jeans and a shirt, wondering why he had not called, looking at her face in the bathroom mirror, applying lipstick and blush, then leaving her silent phone, and the rooms where she lived, and driving to the place they liked.

Witness

THURSDAY DURING THE SCHOOL YEAR is a wheelchair day; they are all wheelchair days, but some more than others. On Thursdays, I drive thirty minutes to Andover, the town where my daughters live. They are Cadence and Madeleine, fourteen and nine. I go to their school and park on the road that goes through the grounds and wait for their classes to end at three-twenty. My right leg hurts when I drive; it hurts when it is not at a ninety-degree angle, and most nights it hurts anyway. While driving, I have to place my foot to the left of the brake pedal and that angle makes my leg hurt sooner, and more. Often my back hurts.

Years ago, I learned that pain and wheelchair fatigue—*sitting*, and worrying about what can go wrong because I can't stand or walk—take most of my energy; I cannot live as normals do, and I must try to do only what is essential each day. So on Thursdays, I neither write nor exercise. I make snacks for my daughters, wrap two ice packs around my leg, drive and wait, then take them to my house for dinner, then back to their house, and then I return to host a writers' workshop at my home. I like Thursdays.

I could leave my house at two-thirty or so, and my leg would not start hurting till after three, my back not till after four, or even later, or not at all. But I try to leave by one-thirty. I bring lunch and a book, and drive to the school. I park and eat a sandwich, drink water, and read. There is no telephone. I have a car phone, which I would not have as a biped. It is harmless. It can ring only when the ignition is on, and no one knows its number; I don't know its number. In the car, I read. The pain starts. At home, the phone rings and rings, and when I am writing, I don't answer; but when I am reading, I feel that I should answer it. But even with the pain, there is peace in the car. The moral torque is that by the time the girls come out of school, the pain is tiring me. I have to be wary of impatience and irritation. A few days ago, I read that a samurai philosophy is to refrain until you can respond instead of reacting. I must work on that.

This fall, in 1996, there is another difficulty: the girls have a dog. And on Thursdays, the dog is alone in the house and by late afternoon it needs to be walked, to relieve itself, be a leashed animal outdoors. So from school, we drive to the house where the girls live with their mother, and they go inside. The house has front steps, so I have never been in it. I would need a man to get me inside, probably three—depending on the men—to go upstairs to the rooms where my daughters sleep. While I wait in the car, I cannot imagine what the girls are doing in the house whose walls and ceilings and furniture and rooms do not exist as images in my mind. Inside, the girls are invisible and soundless; they do not come out with the dog. I admire what I call their anarchy. I cannot make them hurry, not even to a movie or a play, which I tell them will start whether or not we are there; they remain insouciant. I am flesh enclosing tension: we have never been late for a movie or a play. In the car, my leg and back do not admire the girls' anarchy. Patience is leaving, irritation arriving. I read. Then, to my right, I glimpse motion; I look and see the girls finally coming out of the house, the brown short-haired dog ahead of them. Cadence holds the taut leash. The dog is of medium size, young, eager, wagging her tail, sniffing the air. They cross the street behind me. I watch them in the mirror; then they go through a tree line— again they are invisible—and into a large field.

When they disappear, I'm briefly frightened; someone could do something to them. I read, I smoke, sometimes I grunt or moan.

I want the girls to have a dog, and I want them to be happily walking the dog in the field. But I also want my leg to stop hurting. I want to be home with my leg on the wheelchair's leg rest. I want to be there eating dinner with my daughters.

A woman who was my Eucharistic minister, bringing me Communion when I could not go to Mass for more than a year after I got hit, once said to me: "Don't think about what you want; think about what you need." What do I need, sitting in this car? Courage? Patience? I can think only that I need the pain to leave me. My energy is flowing into it. And it is not bad pain. For bad pain, there are good drugs. By now the ice packs are thawed. What I need, waiting for my girls, is for this part of the day to end. It does. After twenty-five minutes or so, they come through the tree line and cross the street and return the dog to their house. Time passes. Then they come out and get into the car and I drive to my home, where a woman I pay is cooking dinner. It is five o'clock. The girls go to Cadence's room and shut the door and play classical music for the potted plants. They study; I answer phone messages, throw away mail, keep what I have to answer or pay. At five-thirty, we eat.

On a Thursday in late October, I drove with my girls from the school to their house. The sky was blue, the air warm, and there were yellow and red autumn leaves; and at the girls' house, to relieve the pain in my leg, I got out of the car. I do this by lowering my wheelchair from a carrier that holds it on the roof. With Joan Didion's *The Last Thing He Wanted*, I got in my chair and went to the front of my car, using it as a shield against the very few moving cars on this street with houses and trees. My leg rested in front of me. Soon it would stop hurting. Two young boys wearing helmets were on skateboards in the road. My daughters have new neighbors across the street. Out of that house came a brown-haired woman in her thirties, carrying a very young boy. She looked at me, then called to the skateboarding boys, told them they could not play in the street. They stalled, pleaded, then skated to the sidewalk. She looked at me again. The boy in her arms wore glasses, and was squirming. The woman came to me, looking down now at my face. She said, "I've been wanting to talk to you for some time. I saw your accident."

"You did?"

"I was with my friend at the call box."

Ten years, three months, and one day before this lovely October afternoon, between midnight and one in the morning, on I-93 north of Boston, I saw a car stopped on the highway. It was a four-lane highway, and the car was in the third lane. There was another car in the breakdown lane, and two women were standing at an emergency call box. Now one of those two women was here, and I felt as

I might if she had told me that long ago we were classmates. We introduced ourselves, shook hands. She said she had just moved to this street and had been talking to neighbors and had realized that I was the man she saw that night. She saw two men hit; the other one died within hours.

She said: "You're an author?"

"Yes."

The boy, not yet three, twisted in her arms, grunted, reached for my wheelchair. His thick glasses made his eyes seem large.

"You were hit by a silver—" She named a car I know nothing about, but not the right one.

I said: "It was a Honda Prelude."

"And it paralyzed you?"

"No. Only my leg's useless. I'm very lucky. I had three broken vertebrae in my back. But my spine was okay. My brain." I felt that I was reciting; as I spoke, I was seeing her at the call box while I drove up to the driver's side of the car that had stopped, the last one I ever walked to. "Where were you coming from?" I asked.

"Joe's American Bar and Grill. My friend and I ate there, and had some drinks."

"The one at the mall?"

After we see a play, my girls and I eat at a seafood restaurant near Joe's, at a mall; I was imagining us doing that, connecting places with this woman standing beside me.

"No. In Boston."

"Where were you going?"

"Andover. I haven't driven the same since that night."

"Neither have I."

The boy was strong and kept turning, lunging, reaching. She said: "I have to get his stroller."

She carried him across the street and into her house, and I sat among fallen leaves near the curb and looked up at yellow leaves and branches and the sky, and saw the woman and her friend at the restaurant, then at the call box. The two skate-boarding boys were not ten years old; since that night, she had borne three sons; and my daughter Madeleine had been born. The woman came out with her son strapped into a stroller and crossed the street. The boy reached for the leg rest of my chair. She said: "He goes to a special school. He sees a lot of kids in wheelchairs."

"What's wrong with him?"

"Probably autism. He's too young for the tests."

He was looking at a book with pictures. Then he started tearing it, its cover too; he tore it in half, then into quarters. He was concentrating, grunt-ing. I said: "He's very strong."

She smiled, and said: "They aren't supposed to be able to tear them."

"He's got a life in there."

"Oh, he does. It's me who's frustrated. Because I can't talk to him. And I know he's frustrated because he can't talk."

The girls came out with their dog and looked at me and the woman, and I said: "Have you met your neighbor?" They came to the sidewalk, and I said: "She was there the night I got hit."

Madeleine looked intently at her; Cadence's mouth opened, and in her cheeks color rose, and she said: "You *were?*"

I saw in her face something that was in my soul, though I did not know it yet; I felt only the curiosity you might feel on hearing an unusual sound in the dark outside your window; Cadence looked as though she had just heard something painful, but it had not yet fully struck her. I introduced the woman and her son to my girls; then they went off with their dog. I looked up at the woman, seeing her beside the highway, watching me fly over the car, land on its trunk. My blood wanted to know; it rushed. She said: "The woman in the broken-down car was running around in the highway."

"She was standing in the speed lane. I was trying to get her off the road." The man who died was her brother.

For a moment, I was there: a clear July night, no cars coming, everything I had to do seeming easy. I said: "I'm glad you had already called the state troopers. They saved my life. I might have bled to death."

"Someone else would have called."

"Maybe. But *after* I was hit."

The boy was trying to get out of his stroller; he reached for my leg rest, for a wheel of the chair, lunged and twisted in the straps.

"I have to take him in," she said.

I wanted to ask her what she saw, but I could not; it was like waiting to confess something, waiting for that moment, for the words to come. When I got hit, I did not lose consciousness, but have never remembered being hit, only flagging down a car for help, then lying on its trunk.

I watched her cross the street with her son and, at her stairs, lift him from the stroller and carry him inside. I began reading again. Soon a car turned the corner behind me and stopped at the woman's house; I watched a man go inside; he was not big, but his shoulders and chest were broad, and he walked with an energy that sometimes saddens me. When my daughters and their dog returned from the field, I moved to my car door, put the leg rest and armrest into the backseat, and got in. Before I raised the wheelchair to its carrier, the man came out of the house, carrying his son, and walked to me. He reached over the wheelchair and we shook hands and exchanged names. His face did not have that serious look of some men, as though all play were gone from their lives, and there was only work, money, the future they may not be alive for. He was a man who could be joyful. I can now see his face more clearly than I see his wife's; when I try to remember her, I see her standing at the call box, a body whose face I could not see in the night.

"My wife said she talked to you."

"It's incredible. I've never met anyone who saw me get hit."

"She called me that night. What's it like for you, after ten years?"

"It's better. I'm used to some things. I still can't drive alone to Boston, at night on Ninety-three."

"Oh, that's a protective device."

"Really? You mean I don't have to think of myself as a wimp?"

"No, no. I believe everything we have is a gift."

We talked about his work, and his son, who was moving in his arms, and he said he'd like to have a beer with me sometime; he would get me up his steps. I told him I would like that. In his face were the sorrow and tenderness of love as he strongly held his writhing son, looking at the small face that seemed feral in its isolation. We shook hands and he went inside.

I started the car, picked up the switch that's attached to a wire on the floor, and pressed it, and the carrier on the roof lowered, two chains with an elongated hook, which I inserted into a slot under the chair's seat. I flicked the switch again, this time in the other direction, and the chains pulled the chair up. But when it reached the frame of the carrier, it stopped. The motor was silent. I released the switch, tried it again. It clicked. The chair did not move. I kept pushing the switch. Its click was disproportionately loud, a sound without promise; yet I kept doing it. The chair was too high for me to reach it and try to take it off the hook, and a thirty-inch metal frame was jutting out from my car.

This is why I have a car phone: for circumstances that require legs. My son-in-law, Tom, is a mechanic. I called him, thirty minutes away in southern New Hampshire. He said he would come. I was calm. I have never been calm when the wheelchair carrier fails, and usually I am not calm for hours after Tom has fixed it. But that day, I was calm, maybe because I had started the day by going to Mass—this always helps—or maybe because my spirit was on the highway on the twenty-third of July in 1986.

I would not have the time to be rescued, then drive my daughters to my house for dinner at five-thirty. My daughters were still inside. When they came out, I told them, and we kissed good-bye, and they went back inside. I phoned the woman at my house, and said we would not need dinner. I read Didion. Tom came in his truck, looked under the hood, worked there for a while, then said it was fixed, for now, but he would have to get a part. My knowledge of things mechanical is very small: pens, manual typewriters, guns. I drove home, feeling that I was on the circumference of a broken circle whose separated ends were moving toward each other. Soon they would meet. Next time I saw her, I would ask everything.

Around seven-twenty, writers began arriving for the workshop, and some of us waited on the sundeck for those still on the road. I told them about the woman and said that next time I would ask her if she saw me get hit; when I heard myself say that, I was suddenly afraid of images I have been spared, and I said no, I would not ask her. We went to the living room, and I told the story again, to the people who had not been on the deck; this time, as I talked, curiosity and wonder left me, as though pushed out of my mouth by the dread rising from my stomach. I looked at the faces of the women and men sitting on the couch, the love seat, the window seat; we formed a rectangle. I was alone at one end. I felt faint, as if I had lost blood. I said: "I think I'll go into a little shock tonight, or tomorrow."

But I was calm that night, and Friday, and Saturday. On Sunday, we had a family dinner with three of my grown children, their spouses, the oldest son's two small children, and Cadence and Madeleine. That morning, the sky was blue, and I was on my bed, doing leg lifts. When I swung my leg and stump up for the fiftieth time, I began quietly to cry. Then I stopped. I made the bed, dressed, ate yogurt and strawberries, showered, dressed on my bed. The tears were gone and would not come back, but my soul was gray and cool, and pieces of it were tossed as by a breeze that had become a strong wind and could become a storm. I drove to the girls' house. They live on the corner of the street, and when I turned onto it, I saw the woman in her yard. She was doing some kind of work, her back was to me, and I looked away from her, at the girls' house, and I phoned them to say, "I'm here."

At my house, we cooked on the grill, and I sat on the deck, my face warmed by the sun, and talked with my children and enjoyed the afternoon. I looked up at my two sons and told them of suddenly crying while doing leg lifts, of being fragile now, and as I talked to them, I made a decision I never make, a decision about writing, because my decisions usually gestate for months, often more than a year, before I try to write anything: I told them I would start writing this on Monday, because meeting the woman, shaking her hand, hearing her voice, seeing her sons, especially the youngest one, and shaking her husband's hand, hearing his witness—*She called me that night*—had so possessed me that I might as well plunge into it, write it, not to rid myself of it, because writing does not rid me of anything, but just to go there, to wherever the woman had taken me, to go there and find the music for it, and see if in that place there was any light.

Next day, I woke to a wind that brought sorrow and fear and rain, while beyond the glass doors in front of my desk the sky was blue, and leaves were red and yellow, and I wrote. For ten days, I woke and lived with this storm, and with the rain were demons that always come on a bad wind; loneliness, mortality, legs. Then it was gone, as any storm. They stop. The healing tincture of time, a surgeon told me in the hospital. On the eleventh day, I woke with a calm soul, and said a prayer of thanks. While I wrote this, the red and yellow leaves fell, then the brown ones, and the nights became colder, and some days too, most of them now in late November, and I did not find the music. Everything I have written here seems flat: the horns dissonant, the drums lagging, the piano choppy. Today the light came: *I'm here.*